As I read through Matt's new [W9-BWR-190] an old Lutheran hymn kept going through my mind: "My hope is built on nothing less than Jesus's blood and righteousness. On Christ the solid Rock I stand. All other ground is sinking sand." In this crazy and changing world, our identity is found while standing on our "Rock," Jesus. I loved reading *I Am* and hearing Pastor Matt open his pastoral heart to lead us into a deeper trust in the unchanging nature of I Am.

—ROBERT BARRIGER
PASTOR, CAMINO DE VIDA (LIFE MISSIONS)
LIMA, PERU

Matt Fry delivers a powerful and compelling message in his new book, *I Am: Encounter the One Who Gives You Purpose and Peace in a Crazy World*. You will be challenged to view yourself, your past, and your purpose in a different light—and ultimately uncover your true identity found in Christ.

—RANDY BEZET
PASTOR, BAYSIDE COMMUNITY CHURCH
BRADENTON, FLORIDA

I believe the biggest challenge most Christ followers face is to be confident in who they are as children of God rather than wishing they were someone different or who others thought they should be. Confidence in your identity is grounded in knowing who God is, not in who you think He might be. In *I Am: Encounter the One Who Gives You Purpose and Peace in a Crazy World*, my good friend Matt Fry helps you solidly understand, from God's perspective, who God really is and subsequently who you are in Him. It's a great read, and I recommend it for anyone who struggles with confidence.

—RICK BEZET
LEAD PASTOR, NEW LIFE CHURCH OF ARKANSAS
CONWAY, ARKANSAS

Having had the privilege of knowing Matt and his wife personally for over fifteen years, I can say that Matt Fry has always been an encourager. In his book, *I Am*, he uses the Word of God, his testimony, and many others' experiences to help you see the plan God has created you to fulfill. Matt is able to make clear the truths found in the Bible so that we can apply them to our lives.

—JOE CHAMPION
PASTOR, CELEBRATION CHURCH
GEORGETOWN, TEXAS

Insecurity. It's probably a leader's number one nemesis. It can cause a leader a whole spectrum of challenges, ranging from existential angst to toxic dysfunction. However, my friend Matt Fry provides the ultimate antidote in *I Am*. Knowing who and whose we are makes that ultimate difference. You will find *I Am* liberating and will want to share it with others.

—SAM CHAND
LEADERSHIP CONSULTANT (WWW.SAMCHAND.COM)
AUTHOR, *LEADERSHIP PAIN*

So many people in this world feel forgotten, abandoned, and alone. They can't remember who they are or what their purpose is. Matt Fry's new book, *I Am: Encounter the One Who Gives You Purpose and Peace in a Crazy World*, reminds us with divine clarity not only who God is but also who we are. This book will help you have an encounter with God and give you powerful tools to fulfill your God-given purpose.

—HERBERT COOPER
PASTOR, PEOPLE'S CHURCH
OKLAHOMA CITY, OKLAHOMA

Matt Fry speaks to an issue that has long been ignored in the church. As followers of Christ we have often championed *how* to live a life of faith. We're even pretty good at explaining *why* we should live a life of faith. Where we come up short is answering the question "Who is a person of faith?"

I Am: Encounter the One Who Gives You Purpose and Peace in a Crazy World offers us a road map, a guidebook to shed light on the eternal identity of a Christ follower. Matt reminds us that a personal relationship with Christ results in a total transformation of who we are!

With intimate glimpses into his own personal struggles, Matt welcomes us to take off the mask, lay down any spiritual facade, and grasp the reality that God loves us and changes us at our core. I'm proud of my younger brother, not just because of the great things he has accomplished, but because of the great man he is! I recommend that you read this book with an open heart.

—Dr. Craig Fry
President, Christian Leadership Concepts
Brentwood, Tennessee

There's a reason Matt Fry pastors an incredible church: he knows how to share God's Word in a way that creates clarity, joy, and peace. Even more, Matt is funny, down-to-earth, and disarming—all of which come through in his amazing book, *I Am*. It can be hard to live in a world filled with doubts and false messages. But *I Am* is a perfect revelation to help us cut through the cultural confusion and give us a divine confidence that our God, "I Am," is greater than all.

—Peter Haas
Pastor, Substance Church
Minneapolis, Minnesota

I Am: Encounter the One Who Gives You Purpose and Peace in a Crazy World provides biblical relief from the countless demands our culture places on us today. Using God's Word as the source for exploring how our Creator views us, Matt Fry reminds us of our status as sons and daughters of the King. With fresh, relevant insight into the way the world attempts to derail our true identity, Matt inspires us not to settle for anything less than God's best for our lives.

—CHRIS HODGES
PASTOR, CHURCH OF THE HIGHLANDS
BIRMINGHAM, ALABAMA

Matt and his wife, Martha, have been faithful, compassionate, genuine lovers of Jesus and builders of the local church for many years. Personable and relatable, Matt has devoted his life to providing people with answers and hope in Jesus through his practical, hands-on teaching style. Be blessed by his vulnerable and personal revelations that the words of Jesus are life, help, and hope to all who hear them.

—BRIAN AND BOBBIE HOUSTON
GLOBAL SENIOR PASTORS, HILLSONG CHURCH
SYDNEY, AUSTRALIA

Pastor Matt Fry has been a voice of passion and authenticity in my life for many years. Having had the privilege of observing his ministry up close and from a distance, I can say Pastor Matt is the real deal. His heart beats to provide real hope for real people in a real world. God has used his voice to refresh and empower many. I have no question that this book will continue to do exactly that. Thank you, Pastor Matt, for writing *I Am* and helping us develop a closer relationship with God.

—JEFF KAPUSTA
PASTOR, LIFEPOINT CHURCH
WILMINGTON, NORTH CAROLINA

In our world today one thing is for sure. If we don't know who we are, then we can never become who we are meant to be. That's why this book is so important. My friend Matt Fry has dialed in a winner here. In bite-size, easy-to-digest chapters, Matt lays out a plain-and-simple guide to discovering who we are and who God has made us to be. Do yourself a favor and get this book!

—MATT KELLER
PASTOR, NEXT LEVEL CHURCH
FORT MYERS, FLORIDA

The overwhelming desire everyone has to know why we were made is clearly and humbly addressed in Pastor Matt Fry's book, *I Am: Encounter the One Who Gives You Purpose and Peace in a Crazy World*. Every day we wrestle with insecurity and often struggle with our true identity in Christ. In this personal and transparent book Pastor Matt identifies what we all need—less *I* and more *I Am*. It's only by embracing and experiencing our full identity in our God that we will overcome the chaos and self-doubt all around us. I strongly recommend this book as a modern-day survival guide for every citizen of the "selfie" age.

—STEVE KELLY
PASTOR, WAVE CHURCH
VIRGINIA BEACH, VIRGINIA

Pastor Matt Fry has an uncanny ability to make complex topics relatable and understandable without losing the importance of what is being discussed. In his book, *I Am: Encounter the One Who Gives You Purpose and Peace in a Crazy World*, he does just that. This work will give you a greater level of hope and faith in the mysterious wonder the great I Am is while building an essential knowledge of tangible effects this awareness can have on us as individuals.

—ROB KETTERLING
LEAD PASTOR, RIVER VALLEY CHURCH
APPLE VALLEY, MINNESOTA

If you have ever struggled with self-esteem issues or have wondered if your life matters, read this book. Matt Fry reveals in *I Am* that you are unique and special, not because of what people say, but because God said so. This book is life-changing!

—BABBIE MASON

Songwriter and recording artist Matt Fry has hit a grand slam with his powerful book, *I Am: Encounter the One Who Gives You Purpose and Peace in a Crazy World*. As you walk with Matt on an exploration of the "I am" statements of Jesus, you will discover as never before the unlimited authority of our Savior and His boundless provision for all who fully follow Him. You will learn as you surrender to the great I Am that He is all you need regardless of your past, your failures, your fears, or your circumstances. In the great I Am you will find your identity, your purpose, and the keys to the abundant life. I highly recommend this outstanding book by a brother who faithfully lives the principles he teaches.

—DOUG CARTER
SENIOR VICE PRESIDENT, EQUIP LEADERSHIP INC.

My new friend Matt Fry has written a most inspiring book about our great I Am. So many of us struggle with knowing our God-given purpose, and we allow so many of our own insecurities and inadequacies to delay our progress. However, with his candidness Matt helps us clearly understand that by encountering the great I Am, we can begin to discover who we are. This book is a must-read, and I am so very proud of the timing of this life-giving message from one of the humblest men I know.

—RAY MCQUEEN
PASTOR, FAMILY LIFE CHURCH
LYNCHBURG AND ROANOKE, VIRGINIA

How easy it is to forget all that God truly is. He is I Am. This book by Pastor Matt Fry will help anyone who reads it set his spiritual compass where it needs to be.

—David L. Meyer
CEO, Hand of Hope

Matt Fry has written an inspiring and anointed must-read! Matt's book reads like a personal conversation with a friend who takes you on a journey through the Scriptures, adding personal stories and experiences to help us discover who God is! Be ready to be challenged, changed, and encouraged by the powerful truth that God is the great I Am!

—Anthony Milas
Pastor, Granite United Church
Salem, New Hampshire

Have you ever asked yourself, "Who am I? Why am I here?" The truth is God has a purpose for your life, and you can discover it by developing an intimate relationship with Him. In Matt Fry's book, *I Am*, he unravels the mystery to finding the destiny God has planned just for you. This book is sure to transform the way you see yourself as you begin to see who you are through God's eyes.

—Robert Morris
Pastor, Gateway Church
Southlake, Texas

The roots of our identity and purpose are only discovered as we grow in our understanding of who Jesus is. Matt's book, *I Am*, will help you uncover more about Christ and the incredible life He has for you to experience.

—Todd Mullins
Senior Pastor, Christ Fellowship
West Palm Beach, Florida

My friend Matt Fry's former college wrestling background has served him well as he back-slams this crucial "identity" truth to the canvas! His refreshingly authentic style will have you not only reading on but also leading better, as he sifts through the mess of the twenty-first century and pulls out a message so relevant to everyone attempting to make sense of this crazy, mixed-up world.

—Pastor Michael Murphy
Founder, Leaderscape
Sydney, Australia

While many books have value, some truly have life-changing value! This book by Pastor Matt Fry is a life-changer. As you read, you'll receive hope and continually be reminded that what has been in your life doesn't determine what can be, and who you have been doesn't determine who you will be in God!

—Dale O'Shields
Pastor, Church of the Redeemer
Gaithersburg, Maryland

Every person struggles with having their identity tied to what they do or what they accomplish. In Pastor Matt's book, *I Am*, you will discover what it really means to understand who Christ is and how that changes the way you view yourself.

—Benny Perez
Pastor, The Church Las Vegas
Las Vegas, Nevada

I love that Matt decided to tackle one of the most crucial—and prevalent—questions people find themselves asking today: Who am I? But what I love most is that he addresses it in the only context that has the power to bring true answers and transformation. He points us back to the One who created us. Matt helps readers dig down and look at some of life's biggest questions in light of God's Word and bring simple truth and practical action steps into this incredibly important conversation taking place in so many people's hearts and minds today.

—JOHN SIEBELING
PASTOR, LIFE CHURCH OF MEMPHIS
MEMPHIS, TENNESSEE

The book you are holding in your hands is an incredible read. As you read through this book, you will laugh, you will think, and most of all you will grow through Pastor Matt's insightful revelation of I Am. This book will inspire you to strengthen your relationship with Jesus regardless of where you are in your faith walk.

—TIM TIMBERLAKE
PASTOR, CHRISTIAN FAITH CENTER
CREEDMOOR, NORTH CAROLINA
AUTHOR, *ABANDON*

Matt Fry knows how to help people find God's plan for their life, and he writes it plainly in this book. He planted C3 Church and has won many of the members to Jesus Christ and helped them find God's plan for their life. Read carefully to receive the help you need.

—DR. ELMER TOWNS
COFOUNDER, LIBERTY UNIVERSITY
LYNCHBURG, VIRGINIA

Pastor Matt Fry's book, *I Am: Encounter the One Who Gives You Purpose and Peace in a Crazy World*, is a phenomenal unpacking of the "I am" statements of Jesus. With so much going on in our culture today, it can be a struggle to discover who we are and what our purpose is. But as you read, Matt shows that we cannot know who we are or what our purpose is until we have a revelation of Jesus. Jesus is the One who makes me who I am. And it is not until we discover who He is that we will discover who we are and what He has called us to.

—CHAD VEACH
PASTOR, ZOE CHURCH
LOS ANGELES, CALIFORNIA

Our world is more confused than ever about identity, but *I Am* reminds us that we cannot know who we are until we know who Jesus is. Matt's timely book unpacks the powerful "I am" declarations Jesus makes in the Gospel of John, which transform the way we understand His nature and the full, satisfying identity He gives us.

—STOVALL WEEMS
PASTOR, CELEBRATION CHURCH
JACKSONVILLE, FLORIDA

ENCOUNTER *the One*

WHO GIVES YOU PURPOSE

AND PEACE IN A

CRAZY WORLD

I Am

MATT FRY

CHARISMA HOUSE

Most CHARISMA HOUSE BOOK GROUP products are available at special quantity discounts for bulk purchase for sales promotions, premiums, fund-raising, and educational needs. For details, write Charisma House Book Group, 600 Rinehart Road, Lake Mary, Florida 32746, or telephone (407) 333-0600.

I AM by Matt Fry
Published by Charisma House
Charisma Media/Charisma House Book Group
600 Rinehart Road
Lake Mary, Florida 32746
www.charismahouse.com

Cover design by Lisa Rae McClure
Design Director: Justin Evans

Visit the author's website at mattfry.com.

Library of Congress Cataloging-in-Publication Data:
Names: Fry, Matt (Pastor), author.
Title: I am / Matt Fry.
Description: Lake Mary : Charisma House, 2017.
Identifiers: LCCN 2017005171| ISBN 9781629991030 (trade paper) | ISBN
    9781629991047 (ebook)
Subjects: LCSH: Identity (Psychology)--Religious aspects--Christianity.
Classification: LCC BV4509.5 .F79 2017 | DDC 248.4--dc23
LC record available at https://lccn.loc.gov/2017005171

17 18 19 20 21 — 98765432
Printed in the United States of America

Contents

Acknowledgments

THANK YOU, C3 Church family, for your passion for God and joining me in fulfilling God's vision to provide real hope for real people in a real world.

Thank you to my amazing wife, Martha, for your support and encouragement.

Thank you, Cara Highsmith and Kimber Liu, for working behind the scenes to help make this book come together.

Foreword

I REMEMBER ATTENDING MY mother's seventieth birthday and being faced with the many different roles I'm asked to play at any given time. Within a span of hours I was characterized by different people in a variety of ways. To one I was my mom's only daughter. To another I was Nick's wife. To another I was Catherine and Sophia's mom. To another I was George's sister, and to my niece I was "the cool aunt who buys all the great presents." Some old friends considered me the "weird one" who had "got religion," and conversely friends from church thought I was a great Bible teacher and author. (OK, I admit they were totally biased but clearly very perceptive!) By the end of the night I was totally exhausted just thinking about all of the different facets that make me *me*.

Just as it is with an actor, playing different parts is a necessary part of our lives, and those roles can change at any given moment. We can easily be pulled in many different directions because of people's demands and expectations on us, but not one of the many roles we play completely defines us. However, that doesn't stop us from trying to define our identity based on those roles rather than on who we are in Jesus Christ. We get all messed up in the process and begin tacking even more things onto our identity— our failures and mistakes, adversity we've faced, and lies we've believed.

I can testify to that firsthand. I was born a statistic— unnamed, unwanted, orphaned. I grew up a bigger statistic—marginalized, abused, and poor. For the first two decades of my life I let those roles and statistics define my identity. But when Jesus found me at the age of twenty-two, I was given a new name—loved and redeemed daughter of God the Father. More than that I met an all-powerful, unchanging God, and that has made all the difference.

The enemy would love to keep us in the dark about the truth of Jesus Christ and who we are in Him. He will use every tool at his disposal to distract us so that we forget who God is, and one of his favorite tools is mistaken identity. The best weapon to combat the enemy's lies is the ever-powerful, unchanging truths of Scripture, and that is why I am so grateful for the message God has given Matt to share in these pages.

It's a game-changer when your identity is found in Jesus rather than in the many roles you play, mistakes you've made, or challenges you've faced. I know Matt to be someone who has personally experienced that life transformation, and he passionately shares the hope and freedom that have come to his life through discovering an identity anchored in Jesus Christ alone.

My prayer for you as you read this book is that you will encounter our heavenly Father on a deeper level, where He will remind you that you too have been given a new name—love and redeemed child of God.

Christine Caine is a respected Bible teacher; a best-selling author; and the founder of Propel, a ministry designed to equip women to fulfill their purpose, and The A21 Campaign, a nonprofit organization dedicated to rescuing victims of human trafficking.

God Is the Great I Am

I STILL REMEMBER THE night I sat on the couch in our living room feeling lost and empty. I honestly didn't know what to do. I had just lost my job and was suddenly struck with the realization that I had lost not only my means of supporting my wife and our two small children but also the status I had enjoyed as part of the staff of a well-known church. As that awareness settled in, I began wrestling with questions about who I really was.

Although there was a lot of noise and activity swarming around me in the house, I felt completely alone. I wondered if God had forgotten about me. I didn't fully realize it at the time, but I was waking up to the harsh reality that my identity—my sense of meaning and purpose—had been connected to my title and position.

It took some time for me to think beyond my emptiness, but as I began to seek God, I discovered that for a lot of my life my sense of worth had been based on what I did.

When I was in high school and college, I was Matt Fry the wrestler. After a decade of serving on a church staff, I was Matt Fry the youth minister. Now I felt like a failure because I was just Matt Fry. I felt as though I had let my family down. And I was angry with God. I had given my life to serve Him, and now I was out of a job. I had surrendered and sacrificed my life for Him, and I thought, "This is what I get?"

For the first time since I had committed my life to Christ, I considered quitting ministry and pursuing a new career. But that would mean starting over in many ways because my degree, training, and experience were in ministry. I couldn't accept that God wanted me to leave the ministry, but I had no clear direction about what I should do next.

I worked for a time as a custodian during the week while traveling on the weekends to speak at churches. One of the places I cleaned was a police station. One night I had to work around a policeman who was sitting at his desk. I said, "Excuse me, sir. Can I get your trash can?" He looked up at me and said, "Don't I know you? Aren't you the youth pastor at the big church down the street?" I said, "I used to be," and awkwardly changed the subject and continued cleaning.

During that time in my life, as I searched God's Word for comfort and direction about what to do with my life, I came across a familiar passage. I had read it many times before, but this time it seemed to jump off the page.

Paul said in Philippians 3:10, I want to know Christ "and the power of His resurrection" (MEV). I thought, "*Yes!*

I want to know Christ and His power!" Then the passage continued, "...and the fellowship of His sufferings" (MEV). I thought, "Can't I have the power without the suffering?" I remember God speaking to me in that moment and saying, "No, Matt, you can't have My power without the suffering." I had to learn they go hand in hand. It's the suffering that brings us the power.

I look back now and realize that losing my job was a defining moment in my life. My paradigm shifted as I went from being Matt Fry the youth pastor who happens to be a Christian to a Christian who was a youth pastor. I stopped linking my significance with my title. By seeking God, I discovered that my identity wasn't in what I did. My identity was found in Him.

Do You Know Who You Are?

One of the biggest challenges we face in this crazy, mixed-up world is answering the question "Who am I?" For some of us, discovering who we are means discovering our destiny. For others, it's about trying to figure out our place in the world and to feel significant.

We struggle to believe we matter, which can cause us to feel completely unworthy. We wonder how God could love us and want to provide for us. And when we don't understand that, it makes everything else we face in life that much harder.

The most fundamental thing we need to know is that no matter what we've done, God is still faithful, and He is good. God loves you, is pursuing you, and still has a purpose for your life even if you've messed up. When I struggle, even when I turn my back on Him, He is still faithful to love me.

There are three things God wants us to be confident of beyond a shadow of a doubt so that we can live out our unique purpose:

- God is good, even when our circumstances are not good.

- God is a great God and has all the power and resources we would ever need.

- God is greater than the enemy, and He gives us the power to overcome the enemy in Jesus's name.

He is an amazing God! God is good, He is great, and He is greater. As 1 John 4:4 says, greater is He who is in me than he that is in the world.

He gives us all the love we will ever need to face every challenge or opportunity we might encounter in our lives. He is so big that we can't completely comprehend all of His attributes, and He knows us intimately down to our smallest details. God knows everything we've done, and He still loves us! Knowing this lays the foundation for having a fresh encounter with God.

We see many examples in the Bible of men and women who had encounters with God. One of the most powerful examples is Moses. He wasn't perfect. In fact, he got in a fight, lost his temper, and killed a man, and as a result he lived as a fugitive in the desert for forty years. It appears that Moses even struggled with insecurity, but God revealed Himself to Moses in an incredible phenomenon.

While in the desert Moses encountered a bush that was on fire but not consumed. And this is where we see God speak to him:

> "Look! The cry of the people of Israel has reached me, and I have seen how harshly the Egyptians abuse them. Now go, for I am sending you to Pharaoh. You must lead my people Israel out of Egypt." But Moses protested to God, "Who am I to appear before Pharaoh? Who am I to lead the people of Israel out of Egypt?" God answered, "I will be with you. And this is your sign that I am the one who has sent you: When you have brought the people out of Egypt, you will worship God at this very mountain."
>
> —Exodus 3:9–12

Instead of accepting this amazing assignment, Moses made excuses. He said: "I am not good enough. I don't have all the answers. People won't believe me. I am a terrible public speaker. I am not qualified." Yet God still chose Moses, not based on what Moses thought of himself, but based on what God could do. Despite Moses's fears, God's plan was for Moses to go to Pharaoh, demand the release of God's people, and lead them out of slavery in Egypt.

As Moses considered this assignment, He asked God:

> If I go to the people of Israel and tell them, "The God of your ancestors has sent me to you," they will ask me, "What is his name?" Then what should I tell them?
>
> —Exodus 3:13

Moses wanted to know God's name. And for the first time in history God actually answered that question. God told Moses:

> "*I Am Who I Am.* Say this to the people of Israel: I Am has sent me to you." God also said to Moses, "Say this to the people of Israel: Yahweh, the God of your ancestors—the God of Abraham, the God of Isaac, and the God of Jacob—has sent me to you. This is my eternal name, my name to remember for all generations."
>
> —Exodus 3:14–15, emphasis added

God is I Am. That is His forever name. He always has been and always will be. He is all you need!

We Need a Fresh Encounter With God

God designed all of us to have a personal relationship with Him and to encounter Him, just as Moses did. Now, you're probably not going to see a burning bush, but the experience will be just as personal for you.

When I experienced a fresh encounter with God, it

changed everything I thought about myself. That's what happened with Moses too. When God spoke to him on the mountain, Moses saw himself as inadequate and unable to be used to set the people of Israel free. But after the encounter, although Moses still had doubts, he saw himself as capable of going before Pharaoh and telling him to let God's people go. After spending time with God, Moses had confidence not in himself, but in the great I Am, who would be with him. Moses's encounter with I Am changed the way he saw himself, and it allowed him to live out God's purpose for his life.

God wants to do the same thing for you! He wants to reveal Himself to you in a personal way so you can discover how He sees you and what He has called you to do. When you have an encounter with the great I Am, you will discover who you are. Here's a statement I want you to remember as we go through this book: when I encounter the great I Am, that's when I begin to discover who I am.

The encounter is where the power is. That encounter might happen through worship. Or it might come through the challenges and trials we face. It can even happen when we question God and ask Him why we are dealing with things in life that don't seem fair. God can handle your doubts and questions. My own questions are what led me to the fresh encounter that helped me realize where my identity was supposed to lie.

In this book we are going to address some important questions that we all have at different times. In God's presence, as we see who He is, we begin to realize who we are—loved, forgiven, redeemed, and called. That's the big idea of this book. We understand who we are by understanding who created us. It's also what helps us live out what God has called us to do and make a difference with our lives.

When we spend too much time frustrated and floundering, we can feel lost and alone, and we end up looking everywhere except to God for answers. But the answer to our problems is not found in having more money, getting our physical needs met, being popular or successful, or gaining more from this world. The key to overcoming our problems is having a fresh encounter with an awesome God!

God Is Still the Great I Am

Think for a minute about that incredible encounter Moses had with God at the burning bush. That's where God gave Moses an assignment that was bigger than anything he had ever considered before. It's where God told Moses He was going to use him to set His people free from slavery in Egypt.

God wants to use you too and do something in your life that is bigger than you can imagine. He is omniscient (all-knowing) and omnipresent (all-present), and He is pursuing you just as He did Moses.

He cares enough about each of us to give us a unique experience reflective of our personal relationship with Him. So though we should desire to encounter God, our goal should not be to seek a specific experience. We don't need to wander the desert looking for another burning bush. All we need to do is seek God. When we seek God, the experience will follow.

As I shared earlier, the three important principles we need to understand are that God is good, God is great, and God is greater. And when we have a fresh encounter with this good, great, and greater God, the same power that Moses experienced is made available to us today so we can overcome!

God is greater than our obstacles.

The people of Israel faced many obstacles that most of us can't even imagine. At the time Moses encountered God at the burning bush, the Jewish people were trapped in slavery and needed to be set free. It looked like a truly impossible obstacle to overcome, but God was working to bring a solution before Moses even knew he had a problem. The same is true of you. Before you encounter your problem, God already has a solution for you. He had been preparing Moses for years to rise up and be the leader the people of Israel needed to get them out of Egypt.

Your assignment may not be to lead thousands of people out of slavery, but God has a special plan for you, and He is capable of removing any obstacle that stands between you and His purposes for your life. No matter what obstacle you may be facing, God is already working on the solution. Rather than focusing on how big your problem is, focus on how big God is, and trust His plans and promises for your life.

God is greater than our insecurities.

The Israelites had been oppressed as slaves of the Egyptians for over two hundred years. There were generations among them that had never known a day of freedom.

Then God appeared to Moses in a burning bush, spoke to him, told him His name, and gave him an assignment. How did Moses respond? He responded with excuses and questions. "What if they don't listen to me? I am not a good speaker. Can You find someone else?"

Moses had to overcome excuses—speaking publicly or going up to Pharaoh and telling him to let all of his slaves go free. But God was patient with Moses and proved Himself to be greater than those fears. When Moses finally listened to God, he was able to overcome the fear and set God's people free.

God will do the same for you if you turn to Him when you feel afraid about what you face in life. It is OK to be fearful when we are going into an unknown situation or when things feel hopeless. But we should never let fear keep us from doing something God is calling us to do because He has promised to bring us through it. (See Isaiah 43:2.)

God is greater than our needs.

The people of Israel faced a long journey after being set free from Egypt. As they made their way through the desert, they faced many challenges in getting to the Promised Land. They set up their own idols and worshipped them. They weren't willing to trust God to meet their needs and had a plan B in case Jehovah God didn't work out. Each time they faced a new challenge—a new need—they forgot how God had provided for them through the last one.

The Israelites couldn't seem to remember that when we seek the great I Am and put Him first, He will take care of our needs. Even though they repeatedly turned their backs on Him, He remained faithful to them and kept His promises.

God keeps His promises to us as well, but we need to seek Him *first*, not second, third, or last. In the Book of Philippians it says, "My God shall supply your every need according to His riches in glory" (Phil. 4:19, MEV). He is sufficient to meet all of our needs, but we have to trust Him to be enough for us.

God is greater than our problems.

After escaping Egypt, the Israelites found themselves in a seemingly impossible situation, with the Egyptian army hotly pursuing them and a big, broad sea spreading in front of them. This was only the first of many problems they would face on the journey, but God made a way through each of them.

One of the greatest things about God is when we feel as if we are up against a brick wall, God can make a way when we feel there is no way. He is greater than any problem we will face because He sees the big picture and He knows the way. My friend Babbie Mason wrote a song called "He'll Find a Way," which reminds us that if God could raise up the mountains, calm the sea, and defeat death, He surely can find a way for you out of whatever struggle you face.

No matter what we are dealing with, no matter what the enemy may throw at us, knowing God is everything we need, and that He is greater than anything we will come up against gives us the courage to keep moving forward. It gives us the security to know that we can overcome. We have the confidence of knowing that God is the great I Am.

If you've ever felt dissatisfied, lost, unfocused, uncertain about who you can trust, powerless, spiritually dry, or disconnected, the answer you seek is in encountering the great I Am. In the Gospel of John, Jesus declares that He is:

The Bread of Life (John 6:35)—the One who satisfies our longings

The light of the world (John 8:12)—the One who shows us the way

The door (John 10:9, KJV)—the One who helps us find what we're really looking for

The Good Shepherd (John 10:11)—the One we can always trust

The Resurrection and the Life (John 11:25)—the One who gives us power

The Way, the Truth, and the Life (John 14:6)—the One who fills us spiritually

The Vine (John 15:5)—the One who helps us connect with Him and others

Getting to know who God is will help us discover who we are in Him. As you look to the One who created us, I believe God will give you a sense of purpose, peace, and the ability to flourish in this crazy world in which we live. Let me encourage you to take this journey in a small group or with your family or a friend so you can discover these life-changing principles together. Take some time after reading each chapter to use the Next Steps to apply what God is speaking to you. You will also notice that each chapter has a declaration for you to speak over your life and others. I encourage you to use those because there is power in declaring the Word of God and in His promises.

I've seen hundreds of lives transformed by getting to know the great I Am. I am confident that as you read this book, God is going to reveal Himself to you in a fresh way, and your life will never be the same.

What we will explore together in these pages will be life-changing. When we understand what God means by saying, "I am," it changes everything. My prayer for you is that as you take this journey with me, you'll personally experience each of these powerful declarations. We serve an amazing God, and as we learn more about the statements He made about who He is, we will also discover the incredible purpose He has for our lives.

Chapter One

Are You Satisfied?

I Am the Bread of Life

I am the bread of life. Whoever comes to
me will never be hungry again. Whoever
believes in me will never be thirsty.
—JOHN 6:35

HAVE YOU EVER seen the TV show *Man v. Food* on
the Travel Channel? In each episode the host of the show,
Adam Richman, takes on a food challenge. It's like he's in
his own one-man eating competition. He travels around
the country visiting different cities and trying out food for
which the area is known. Sometimes he eats spicy food
made with super-hot peppers, or he'll stuff down a restaurant's "big food" feature, such as a five-pound burger or a
seventy-two-ounce steak. And what's most amazing to me

is that no matter how much Adam Richman eats, he still manages to make room to eat again in the next episode.

The show makes me think of when I was a wrestler in high school. At the end of the season my mom took me out to eat lunch and let me pick the restaurant. I chose one of those all-you-can-eat pizza places and stuffed down about twenty-one slices of pizza. I was so full that all I could do was lie down and moan in pain. I didn't think I would want to eat again for days. Nor did I think eating a slice of pizza would sound like a good idea ever again, for the rest of my life. But I actually was hungry later that night, and I've definitely eaten quite a bit of pizza since then.

Whether it is with food, possessions, money, or relationships, we all have this tendency to try to fill our lives with things that we think might help us feel fulfilled. We pack our schedules with work and activities. We stuff our homes (and sometimes storage spaces for the overflow) with junk we don't really need—and none of it ever satisfies our real hunger.

CAN'T GET NO SATISFACTION?

One of The Rolling Stones' first big US hits was a song called "(I Can't Get No) Satisfaction." That song continues to be popular because it speaks to a need in our culture. So many people are trying to find satisfaction in this world but keep coming up empty.

Maybe you can relate. You've tried to find satisfaction in a relationship, but the person lets you down. Maybe you've tried to satisfy your emptiness through drugs or alcohol, but they leave you empty and needing more. Perhaps you've tried to get satisfaction through success, money, or status, but they provide only temporary results.

The reality is none of these provide long-term or eternal satisfaction. But there is good news. Jesus offers us a kind of comfort, enrichment, and fulfillment that will sustain us!

True Worship

Jesus is the only one who can truly satisfy, but we should never serve Him *because of what He can do for us*. Jesus wants us to worship Him for who He is, not what we can get from Him.

When I lost my job and I was so scared about the future, I was really tempted to stay angry with God because it seemed He had not done His part. I had committed my life to serving Him only to end up unemployed with a growing family to support. I thought I was supposed to be blessed since I had given my life to serve God in ministry for the rest of my life. When I didn't know how I would provide for my family, I began to wonder where God was. Why had He not shown up in my hour of need?

I had almost started viewing God like Santa Claus and got mad when I didn't find under the tree what I expected to see on Christmas morning. Maybe you know the feeling. Perhaps you've fallen into the trap of thinking Jesus is supposed to be a wish granter rather than a peace giver. God's heart is for us to pray like His children who love Him, not like beggars who just want Him to meet their needs.

Rather than begging or complaining, we should be

thanking Him. Too often, even when we remember to pray, we don't begin our prayers with words of praise. We're so focused on our needs that we don't take the time to first thank God for how far He has brought us on the journey and for the work He's done that we just don't see yet. Instead, we start our conversations with God by complaining about everything that isn't going right.

Have you been rejecting God because you feel He hasn't done more to help you with your challenges or needs in life? I certainly did at one time in my life. But if I had stayed in that mind-set, I never would have realized the blessings that were to come. In most cases we don't get the privilege of knowing definitively what God has in store for us. That's why we have to trust Him, His goodness, and His love.

When I was able to turn to His Word and start praising Him for all He is and every way He had guided and loved me up to that point, it didn't take long for me to release my fears about providing for my family and find hope for my future, even though I couldn't see where we were headed.

God took me to verses such as John 6:26–27, in which Jesus said:

> I tell you the truth, you want to be with me because I fed you, not because you understood the miraculous signs. But don't be so concerned about perishable things like food. Spend your energy seeking the eternal life that the Son of Man can give you. For God the Father has given me the seal of his approval.

Scripture passages such as this one helped me understand that Jesus wants a relationship with us that remains consistent through the good and the bad. He wants us to call on Him to celebrate with us when things are going well and to help and comfort us when we are having a hard time.

God is the great I Am. He's a holy God and worthy of our praise all the time, not just when He blesses us! He loves it when we worship Him simply for who He is.

God wants to work miracles in our lives. Contrary to how it may feel sometimes, God isn't entertained by seeing us struggle and endure sadness, disappointment, or pain. It gives Him joy to see us growing, thriving, and leading rewarding lives, but that's not why we worship Him. That's not why we serve Him. We don't serve Him because of what we can get from Him, but because we love Him.

You might find you are tempted to worship God only during the good times, to worship Him only when things are going the way you want. It is important to understand that true worship is praising Him even when we can't see the work He is doing in our lives. It is thanking Him for how He has already equipped us to take on what we are facing and what is to come. Worship is trusting that what He has planned for our lives is never for our harm.

> *Yet a time is coming and has now come when the true worshipers will worship the Father in the Spirit and in truth, for they are the kind of worshipers the Father seeks. God is spirit, and his worshipers must worship in the Spirit and in truth.*
> —John 4:23-24, NIV

Worship is sitting in the love He wraps us in and letting that feed our souls and fulfill our every need.

Faith, Not Works

After serving as a youth pastor for many years, I found myself at a crossroads. A Virginia church-planting organization asked me to consider starting a church somewhere in that state. After traveling all over Virginia, my wife and I decided to start a church in Chesapeake. We had the name, the vision, the strategy, the timeline, and the budget all laid out. It was an exciting prospect—the kind every young pastor wants—because there were a number of families already on board, and there was funding for the church to get up and running. It made perfect sense and was a great opportunity.

As we were going through the final process, I was contacted by my father-in-law, who told me about a group of about fifty people in the Cleveland community near Clayton, North Carolina, who were trying to plant a church in that area. He asked if I would talk with them. So I drove down to North Carolina and sat in a Cracker Barrel and talked with them about what I was going to do with this new church in Virginia. I shared my vision, strategy, timeline, and all I was believing God for. They said what I described was exactly what they wanted to do in Clayton.

This small group had been meeting in an elementary school and had no budget to give me a salary. I just didn't see how it was the right move for me to make. I came away from the meeting wishing them well and planning to head back to Virginia to continue with my plans. My father-in-law and I agreed that it didn't make sense on paper, and I think the people I met with knew they couldn't ask me to come to Clayton without really having anything to offer me.

However, when I got back home, I couldn't shake the feeling that I was supposed to go to Clayton—despite the fact that on its face Clayton didn't look like a good choice. Everything in my mind was shouting that it was a bad idea, and I even had a mentor tell me he thought the venture in North Carolina was just too risky. But everything in my heart was telling me that was where God wanted me.

After Martha and I prayed about it, we became even more convinced that North Carolina was where God wanted us. Even though Martha was pregnant with our third child and we had no clue what would be waiting for us in North Carolina, we ended up going to Clayton. But our step of faith did not come without challenges.

The school where we met only allowed us access to certain parts of the building. We held services for the adults in the "cafetorium," and the children had to meet in the hallways because we weren't allowed to use the classrooms.

But by our stepping out in faith, God grew our congregation. On that first Sunday I looked out and saw fifty people but had a vision for a full space, and a few weeks later God made that vision a reality. Three years later we were stepping out in faith again when God provided thirty-three acres where we could build our own twenty-thousand-square-foot facility.

We trusted in the kingdom principle that we reap what

we sow, and we found that while the work we did wasn't unimportant, God was more interested in the fact that we trusted Him to take our work and multiply it. We knew that if we did what He asked us to do, even though it might not have made a lot of sense, He would turn it into something beyond our expectations.

We have learned over and over that God blesses us in ways we can't even see when we step out in faith and trust Him, just as Jesus instructed:

> They replied, "We want to perform God's works, too. What should we do?" Jesus told them, "This is the only work God wants from you: Believe in the one he has sent."
>
> —John 6:28–29

God honors us when we take steps of faith. God honors us when we pray in faith, serve in faith, and reach out to others in faith. The devil wants you to think you aren't making a difference. Remember that God's results look a lot different from the results we see because we don't have heaven's view. You never know how God is going to use the seed you sow.

Action doesn't lead to faith; faith leads to action.

Action doesn't lead to faith; faith leads to action because faith requires acting even when we can't see what lies ahead. The Bible says:

> What good is it, my brothers and sisters, if someone claims to have faith but has no deeds?

Can such faith save them? Suppose a brother or a
sister is without clothes and daily food. If one of
you says to them, "Go in peace; keep warm and
well fed," but does nothing about their physical
needs, what good is it? In the same way, faith by
itself, if it is not accompanied by action, is dead.

—JAMES 2:14–17, NIV

Do you want your marriage to be healthy and flourish?
It takes hard work. You have to serve your wife when you
are tired, and she still has to be willing to listen when she's
mad. Sometimes you have to act first out of commitment,
and feelings come later. You'll be amazed at the change
in attitude that can happen when you do something for
someone even though you don't feel like doing it.

Do you want your finances to be blessed instead of in
a mess? Then do something proactive. Start putting God
first in your giving. The Bible tells us to give God our first-
fruits. He wants us to give back to Him the first 10 percent
of our income, which is called a tithe. It all comes from
Him in the first place! You can go through Dave Ramsey's
Financial Peace University or make a budget and stick to
it. Neither of these will be a miraculous cure or a quick fix,
but they will get you moving in the right direction and
focused on the right things so God has a chance to work
in your life.

Do you want to find a godly wife or husband? You have
to stop worrying about whom you will marry and focus
on building healthy relationships based on God's Word.

Instead of worrying about when you'll find Mister or Miss Right, work on yourself. Are you the type of person you would want to marry? Being content in who you are in Christ provides a confidence that enables you to stop worrying about whom you will date or marry. When we focus on God and His calling for our lives, He can bring someone our way who is running in the same direction.

Do you want to be healthy? Our being healthy starts on the inside and flows out. As our soul is healthy, the Bible says our body will be healthy: "Beloved, I pray that you may prosper in all things and be in health, just as your soul prospers" (3 John 2, NKJV). Good health takes more than just laying off the donuts and using the latest exercise machine. There are no magic pills, miracle diets, or secret treatments that are going to take the work out of getting and staying healthy.

Do you want to change the world? It takes more than just wishing things would be different. It starts with seeing a need where you are and working to fix it. Then, piece by piece and person by person, you'll notice a difference. If we all do that where we are, God can use us to accomplish amazing things. We have to step out in faith, take up our crosses daily, and follow Jesus!

Let's join together in faith to affect the world together! You have to step out in faith before you see any change!

Only Jesus Can Satisfy

As we consider what we really hunger for and how God can meet that need, we should look at the "I am" declaration Jesus gives in the Gospel of John:

> Jesus replied, *"I am the bread of life.* Whoever comes to me will never be hungry again. Whoever believes in me will never be thirsty. But you haven't believed in me even though you have seen me. However, those the Father has given me will come to me, and I will never reject them. For I have come down from heaven to do the will of God who sent me, not to do my own will. And this is the will of God, that I should not lose even one of all those he has given me, but that I should raise them up at the last day. For it is my Father's will that all who see his Son and believe in him should have eternal life. I will raise them up at the last day."
>
> —John 6:35–40, emphasis added

Jesus said, "I am the bread of life." That means He is the One who provides for us and really satisfies. When we fill our lives with things and focus on trying to meet our physical needs, we will inevitably get hungry again; we will get thirsty again. Those needs will keep coming back up and won't ever be permanently satisfied.

Jesus had just performed an amazing miracle through the disciples, feeding five thousand men with just a couple of fish and five loaves of bread. They found a boy with a small lunch who was willing to share, and God multiplied it. Not only did He make sure everyone there was fed, but also He provided so much abundance out of that small gift that they had twelve baskets of leftovers.

There are a few important things to notice in that story. First, we see that God does exceedingly and abundantly more than we could ask for or imagine (Eph. 3:20). Sure, He could have reproduced just enough to make sure everyone had lunch, but as if that miracle weren't impressive enough, He made sure there were leftovers for later.

We also see through this event that while basic needs—such as having food and shelter—are of major concern to us, they are not a big deal for God. We get so wrapped up in making sure our basic physical needs are met and worrying about how we're going to cover them. Yet God is saying, "Look, I've got this covered! And just to show you how insignificant it is, I'm going to give you more than you asked for—by a lot!"

God's focus is on feeding us spiritually and helping us grow closer to Him. Jesus took care of the crowd's physical hunger so He could move on to feeding their spiritual hunger. Even His disciples were more concerned about how to provide food for everyone who had gathered than they were about what Jesus would tell them about who He is and the healing He offers.

This miracle of provision set the stage and set expectations for His ministry that had some troubling fallout. After Jesus fed the multitude, word got around, and everyone, including His disciples, became more focused on *what* Jesus could do for them than *who* He is.

You may be thinking it was all smooth sailing once I decided to step out in faith and go where God was calling me to go. That's not exactly how it went down. There were many ups and downs, from relational challenges to logistical obstacles. I mentioned how we bought land three years after launching, but it wasn't just because we were growing, although we were, and it was awesome to see God working in the community.

We had a quarterly rental agreement with the elementary school where we met, and they reached a point where they decided we couldn't use their facilities any longer. That gave us three months to find a new home! Can you imagine? Some of our members wanted to fight it and assert our rights as taxpayers, but I knew we just needed to trust God to guide us in our next steps.

When you continue to face difficulties as you are doing what you believe God has called you to do, it is normal to question whether you really made the right decision. I can remember initially feeling some panic. What would we do? There was no building to rent in this unincorporated community. We would have to relocate our church ten miles away or find land. But we felt God had called us to this community, so we trusted Him to provide land for us.

When we found a thirty-acre piece of property, I really felt it was what God wanted for us. Our congregation prayed and fasted. After church one Sunday we walked the property and joined hands in prayer. We claimed the property in Jesus's name! Then we submitted an offer, which was really more than we could afford.

They turned us down and wouldn't even counteroffer! I was discouraged and embarrassed because we had stepped out in faith, and it didn't work out. Soon after, I was spending time with God, and He spoke to me. It wasn't just audible; it was loud and so clear. God said, "Matt, I am going to provide land for you. And it's going to be even better than the land you wanted."

That's when I started getting excited. Where would it be located? Not too long after that we found a piece of property that was an old tobacco field. It wasn't even for sale, but God touched the owner's heart, and he sold it to us. After eating a Bojangles' biscuit, the owner and I drove to the property that wasn't for sale, and I said, "Now, can't you see a church on this property?" He looked at me and said, "Yes, Matt, I can." That was the beginning of the miracle.

Not one to quit while I was ahead, I asked him to give the property to us! He said, "I wish I could. But what I can do is owner-finance it with 0 percent interest." We call it the miracle on a tobacco field. We initially bought thirty-three acres and later bought fourteen more. Now we have a forty-seven-acre campus with one hundred thousand square feet that God has provided for us!

This is an example of how you have to be careful not to fall into the trap of forcing your own solutions or demanding miracles from God. We see this in the crowd that had gathered around Jesus in Capernaum:

> They answered, "Show us a miraculous sign if you
> want us to believe in you. What can you do? After
> all, our ancestors ate manna while they journeyed
> through the wilderness! The Scriptures say, 'Moses
> gave them bread from heaven to eat.'"
>
> —John 6:30–31

Jesus responded:

> "I tell you the truth, Moses didn't give you bread
> from heaven. My Father did. And now he offers
> you the true bread from heaven. The true bread of
> God is the one who comes down from heaven and
> gives life to the world."
>
> "Sir," they said, "give us that bread every day."
>
> Jesus replied, "I am the bread of life. Whoever
> comes to me will never be hungry again. Whoever
> believes in me will never be thirsty."
>
> —John 6:32–35

The devil will never stop throwing temptations and distractions in our paths. The Bible says he has come to steal, kill, and destroy. But Jesus says He came to give us life! (See John 10:10.)

No matter how much of this world you consume, it's going to leave you empty. Going back to my experience with the pizza at the beginning of the chapter, it doesn't matter how much you cram down your throat in one meal; you will always get hungry again. No matter how much you plan, there will always be some detail overlooked. There will always be another bill to pay, something else that will break down and need repairs.

It is equally important to understand that God will provide for all of our needs, yet we should not treat Him as an ATM. It may seem contradictory to say, "Turn your cares over to God, but don't ask Him for too much." It's not contradictory when you realize that Jesus is the Bread of Life. What Jesus is offering will satisfy us for a lifetime. When we understand and embrace that, the rest of the stuff is not a concern because we trust Him to make sure we have what we need.

Pat's Story
Only Jesus Satisfies

When I was growing up, we didn't have a Bible in our home, though we did go to a Catholic church in the small town where we lived. I went to the confirmation classes and took my first Communion but really didn't know what it all meant. I just remember the statues of Jesus hanging on the cross, the sculptures of Mary, and all the ornate design of the church.

After I got married and had children, I periodically went to a Baptist church and sent the kids with my sister-in-law to her church, but we didn't attend much as a family. One day a friend asked me to go to Bible study with her. I was excited to finally have some structure in my learning about Jesus and to understand what I was reading in the Bible. Unfortunately, church leaders told me I couldn't keep coming to the Bible study because I wasn't a member of that church, and no one invited me to join.

While I was living in Maine, the snow would get so heavy that you had to keep your roof cleaned off. In 1995 after a big snowstorm I was shoveling snow off our roof. My husband, Paul, had been disabled by a work accident, so I took on all the chores he normally did while working a full-time job. Exhausted, I sat down in the thigh-high snow and cried. I looked up and said, "God, I just can't do this anymore." Little did I know, God already had a plan for my family.

The company I worked for opened stores in North Carolina, and we took a leap of faith to move, leaving behind lifetime friends and family. We settled in the Raleigh area and decided to look for a church. We went to a large church near our home and were overwhelmed; it wasn't very inviting. We ended up finding out about C3 Church holding services in an elementary school. To be honest, I was a little turned off by the fact that they didn't even have a building.

We decided to go anyway, and from the minute I walked into C3, I felt so welcome there. I was amazed by the teens who sat in front of us, worshipping with their hands held high—this was new to us. God began to stir in my heart, and I realized that it wasn't the building that made a church, and that wasn't what would satisfy the need I had in my soul. Paul and I joined a connect group, and I didn't have to be a member to join. There was no pressure, and it was OK if I didn't know where to find the scripture in the Bible. There were other people there in the same place I was starting in my walk, and we learned together.

Soon after we started attending, Pastor Matt asked Paul if he wanted to be baptized. Paul felt he was ready and asked me if I would be baptized with him. I told him that I had been "sprinkled" and didn't need that. As the week went on, I continued to read my Bible and pray. During that time I felt God's quiet nudging to be baptized too, so Paul and I were baptized in a swimming pool. Our life has never been the same—the old is gone.

I started volunteering in the office, and soon Pastor Matt asked me to come on staff, and I continued to serve Pastor Matt and Martha as our little church grew with real hope for real people. I was one of those real people who needed real hope, and through that hope I have discovered that God does satisfy every need we have.

I am thankful that Paul and I walked into that elementary school to find Jesus and our church family.

Pat struggled for many years trying to make ends meet and searched in the wrong places for answers. It wasn't until she really sought a relationship with God that she found the fulfillment and peace she had been looking for. You're probably wondering how to know if you're satisfied. Ask yourself, "Do I get stressed about my needs being met?" If so, Jesus wants to reveal Himself to you as the Bread of Life. When you have Jesus, you can set aside all the worries that distract you from focusing on what God wants you to do and where He wants you to use your gifts because He will meet all your needs in His time and in His way. He truly satisfies.

NEXT STEPS

Read Ephesians 3:20–21:

Now to him who is able to do immeasurably more than all we ask or imagine, according to his power that is at work within us, to him be glory in the church and in Christ Jesus throughout all generations, for ever and ever! Amen.

—NIV

Reflect:

- What does this verse say God can do?

- What are some things you are asking God for?

- Do you believe He can do immeasurably more than you can ask or imagine? Why or why not?

Declare:

God, You are doing more than I am asking or can imagine. Your power is working in me to accomplish the plans and purposes You have for me!

Chapter Two

Do You Feel Lost?

I Am the Light of the World

I am the light of the world. If you follow me,
you won't have to walk in darkness, because
you will have the light that leads to life.
—John 8:12

*N*OT TOO LONG ago my son told me about a new game
for my iPhone called Pokémon Go, and I thought it would
be fun to download it so I could connect with my son and
his friends. A lot of youths and young adults seem to be
consumed by it. The game presents an alternate reality that
allows you to see the street or room around you through
the camera on your phone, and little cartoon monsters
pop up that you wouldn't see otherwise. So I installed the
app on my phone, and my son and I wandered around

our neighborhood looking for fictional creatures called Pokémon to capture. It was a pretty fun game, except I noticed that at one point we had nearly wandered into our neighbor's yard without even realizing it!

Apparently lots of people were having this problem. Guided by their phones, they head off after various types of Pokémon, perhaps a Pikachu or something. But because they aren't paying attention to where they are really going, they find themselves in unexpected places. There have been reports of people wandering into traffic or off cliffs. It is unbelievable how lost they can get when they have their heads down, following a guidance system that isn't taking into account the reality around them.

There have been times in my life when I thought I knew where I was headed and what I was supposed to be doing, only to end up disappointed because my expectations didn't pan out. I was convinced I was on the right path because I was pursuing something in front of me that looked real. But I was chasing something that wasn't actually put in my path by God. I was truly lost and overwhelmed when I realized just how far off course I'd gotten.

Do You Know Where You're Going?

Can you relate? Do you feel as if you are wandering aimlessly in life? Are you having a hard time finding something to lead you in the right direction? When we feel lost, we can easily go chasing after other people or possessions, but they won't necessarily lead us toward safety and freedom. There is one person you can trust to lead you in the right direction. Jesus has declared that He is the Light, and you can trust Him to lead you down the right path.

Follow the Light

When I was a teenager, I went spelunking in a cave with my Boy Scout troop. In other words, we crawled on our hands and knees through tunnels and squeezed through narrow crevices until the cave opened up into a big cavern. It was damp and dark, and we had no clue what to expect around the next corner. Part of the adventure included spending the night inside the cave. Now, as inexperienced "explorers" each of us had a helmet with a flashlight attached to the front to help us find our way without facing too much danger, so it didn't seem all that scary. But once we settled where we would camp for the night and it was time to go to bed, our guides made us turn off our lights.

Since we were in a cave and there was no light peeking in from the moon and stars, and there was no source of artificial light, it was pitch-black. I couldn't even see my hand in front of my face. It was pretty eerie to feel so alone and away from everything. I was as blind as I could be and still have my sight.

In the years since my adventure in the cave there have been times when I have felt lost and didn't know what to do. Right now you may be feeling that way—as if you are in a cave in life and having a hard time finding something to light your path and show you the way out. When we find ourselves in darkness, it can be easy to gravitate toward any light we see, hoping it will lead us where we want to be.

We have to be careful because whom we are following determines where we are going, and where we are going determines our destiny. You don't have to have your future figured out, but you do need to be clear on whom you are following toward that future.

We learn in basic science classes that darkness is the absence of light, and this world can be a very dark place.

Whom we are following determines where we are going, and where we are going determines our destiny.

It can feel crazy and mixed up, causing people to walk in darkness because the "light" they are following isn't the light of Jesus. But how do we discern what we are supposed to follow when we feel surrounded by darkness? How do we locate the way out when everything around us is so black we can't even see our hands in front of our faces?

The great thing is that in God's presence we will find all the light we need because He *is* the light.

There are three things that people tend to seek when they are lost. The enemy used these three things when he tempted Adam and Eve in the Garden of Eden. He tried to use these things again with Jesus in the Garden of Gethsemane. And he still tries to lure us with these same temptations today. They are pleasure, power, and possessions. Or you could call them lust, pride, and greed.

When we follow Jesus as the light rather than the things of this world, He actually provides us with all three in ways that fulfill our lives rather than destroy them, as the following verses attest:

- Pleasure: "Take delight in the Lord, and he will give you your heart's desires" (Ps. 37:4).

- Power: "But you will receive power when the Holy Spirit comes upon you. And you will be my witnesses, telling people about me everywhere—in Jerusalem, throughout Judea, in Samaria, and to the ends of the earth" (Acts 1:8).

- Possessions: "Seek the Kingdom of God above all else, and live righteously, and he will give you everything you need" (Matt. 6:33).

We Have the Light

One of the hardest things for most of us guys to do is admit when we are lost. One night I was driving my youngest daughter to a friend's house for a sleepover, and I put the address in my GPS. We started off in the right direction, but the next thing I knew, we were on a dirt road in the middle of the country. The road came to a dead end, and in front of us was an old house with a large dog on a chain barking and growling at us.

I immediately started praying as I put the **Jesus is the** car in reverse, trying desperately to get out of **light that** there before we ended up in a horror film sce- **leads to life.** nario. I had visions of a man coming out of his house with a shotgun, asking, "Why are you on my property, boy?" and not waiting for an answer before starting to fire.

We raced through the dust cloud I'd stirred up with my spinning wheels and headed back in the direction we'd come from. When we got back out to the main road, my daughter looked at me as if she was wondering if she'd ever get to her friend's house. I was beginning to wonder if we'd see civilization again. So I had to humble myself and stop at an old country store and ask for directions.

Eventually we made it to the right house, but we wasted a lot of unnecessary time being lost when I could have just asked someone to show me the way.

I had the same kind of shortsightedness when I was pursuing my own interests in life. I told myself I was doing what God called me to do, but when I saw an opportunity, I did not spend time in prayer or studying God's Word to be sure He wanted me to pursue that prospect. I told myself it was God's plan, but I never actually *asked* God if it was what He wanted because I was being selfish and pushing for something I wanted.

What I didn't realize at the time was that God had something much greater in store for me. It may not have had as much prestige, but I couldn't imagine how it would impact the lives of so many who may not have been reached otherwise. It took prayer and searching my Bible—asking for directions—for me to understand that even though I was seeking God, I was being shortsighted about where I thought I should be serving Him.

The Bible also tells us in Psalm 119:105, "Your word is a lamp to guide my feet and a light for my path." God's Word guides us along the path we should take and illuminates pitfalls along the way that we need to avoid. If we aren't in the Word, we can wander into darkness because we don't know what lies ahead. This is why we need the light that comes from Jesus. Since Jesus is the light, and He is in us, we have the light.

Through the light of Jesus we will see things others can't see as God reveals what He wants us to know when we need to know it. Part of the reason He does this is because He needs us to trust Him to lead. And another part of the reason is that if we have an idea of what's before us, we may try to run ahead and get there before we are ready. Following God instead of trying to direct from behind will get us where we need to be in the most successful way possible.

WE SHINE THE LIGHT!

I traveled to Sweden some time ago to speak at a church. While there I learned that from May until late August, it is light well into the night. You can go to bed around midnight, and the sun will still be shining. During that time of year, it's only dark from around 1:00 a.m. to 4:00 a.m. But the opposite is true if you go during the winter. In some of those months, it's dark almost twenty-four hours a day.

> **I will keep you and will make you to be a covenant for the people and a light for the Gentiles, to open eyes that are blind.
> —Isaiah 42:6–7, NIV**

In parts of the world where there is virtually no sun for months at a time, there is a lot of depression, and suicide rates go up during the months when there is no light. Why? There is just something so powerful about the light. Doctors

41

even prescribe light therapy to help supplement what people aren't getting from the sun, or as an addition to antide-pressants.[1] It also helps with other physical ailments. The healing power of physical light is undeniable, so imagine how much more restoration comes from the supernatural light of Jesus! We are called to be a reflection of that light.

You might be thinking, "People are supposed to look to me for light? There is no way I can guide someone else! I can't even find my own way." Well, look at it this way: We all like candles because they create a warm glow that isn't really harsh and doesn't make the room too bright. But did you know the light of a candle can be seen up to twenty miles away? Your life can and will have an impact far beyond what you imagine.

People get discouraged when they walk in darkness. That's why Jesus had to come and bring the light to us! The Feast of Tabernacles was taking place when Jesus said in John 8:12, "I am the light of the world. If you follow me, you won't have to walk in darkness, because you will have the light that leads to life." This feast was an eight-day celebration during which the Israelites thanked God for guiding them through the wilderness with a cloud by day and a pillar of fire by night.

The rabbis would dance around four candelabras, and then they would put them out at the end of the festival. They used physical light to symbolize the light of wisdom, knowledge, hope, and life that comes from God.[2]

The Jews were reflecting on what God had done for their ancestors—which is an important thing to do—but they were missing the fact that God was willing to give them the light of life that day! Jesus wants to give us that same hope and light for today and the future!

When we feel lost, we can either follow Jesus in the light, or we can follow the darkness of this world. When Jesus is in you, you are a light to the world because He is the light of the world!

WE CAN BE THE LIGHT

We all know that the moon doesn't produce light on its own; it just reflects the light of the sun. When we shine the light of Jesus, it is different because we don't just *reflect* the light of Jesus. When He is in us, His light shines through us out to the world.

We aren't just capable of showing His light, though. We are called to share it with the world, as we see in the Book of Matthew:

> You are the light of the world. A town built on a hill cannot be hidden. Neither do people light a lamp and put it under a bowl. Instead they put it on its stand, and it gives light to everyone in the house. In the same way, let your light shine before others, that they may see your good deeds and glorify your Father in heaven.
>
> —MATTHEW 5:14–16, NIV

This instruction is one of the most intimidating things God tells us to do. Many believers have no problem loving

God, praising Him, and even obeying Him. But when it comes to going out and telling others about Him, we clam up. The good news is that there are a lot of different ways to show the light of Jesus within us that don't involve preaching.

Being the light with our attitude

Some time ago we had a TV crew from New York City visit our campus to film a reality show. When the producer of the show walked into our lobby, she said she could feel something. She was not a believer and not really familiar with the church, but she said she felt peace there. She got emotional and talked about what a tough day she'd had and said she just wanted to stay right where she was.

> Preach the gospel wherever you go, and when necessary use words.
> –Author Unknown

That was an answer to our prayer that our church wouldn't just be a place that has a worship service every week, but would be a place where lives would be impacted seven days a week. We want people to come on our campus and feel the love and peace of Jesus!

The Scripture says people don't light a lamp and put it under a bowl (Matt. 5:15). As followers of Jesus and as a church we are told to let the light within us shine for everyone to see and experience. Our attitudes are a big part of communicating that light. As the old saying goes, for some people, you may be the only Bible they read, so make sure what you are conveying is the love and light that comes from Jesus.

Being the light with our actions

One of our values at C3 is "we serve." We have an outreach ministry called Project 919, which helps reach out and serve the 919 area code, which includes the Raleigh, Durham, and Johnston County areas. We feel a responsibility to share the love of Jesus with those around us, and we feel it is important to just be good neighbors. For us, one of the most powerful actions we can take to show the love of Jesus is to serve others.

Serving our community, helping it to grow, and providing a safe and stable environment for the people who live here are part of what we feel God wants us to do. Our Project 919 ministry allows us to partner with our community to offer support and empower people who are struggling to reach their greatest potential. That support might be providing food or clothing, helping with home repairs, or meeting other basic needs. It's basically being the hands and feet of Jesus.

James 1:22 says, "Be doers of the word and not hearers only" (MEV). Our actions are some of the most effective ways to shine the light of Jesus into the world. We shine the light by responding to others in love rather than reacting in anger and bitterness. We shine the light by proactively showing others the love of Jesus. "Let your light shine before others, that they may see your good deeds and glorify [our heavenly Father!]" (Matt. 5:16, NIV).

Being the light with our generosity

Giving is not all that difficult to do, and there are plenty of people who make charitable contributions for tax deductions or to make themselves feel better around the holidays. And don't get me wrong—those contributions, in the right hands, have a huge impact on people in need, whether locally or globally. But that's different from generosity. Giving is a part of generosity, but it is only the action part, not the heart part. Generosity is about giving because you feel blessed and want to share that with others. It's about showing those who may not know that the work God is doing in your life is also available to them. That is what motivates us in our programs such as Project 919.

The world's values can be pretty selfish: get all you can, can all you get, and sit on the can. We have to fight against that tendency and make an effort to be generous. The gospel is all about giving. Jesus is all about generosity. He gave His life for us! Proverbs 22:9 says, "Blessed are those who are generous, because they feed the poor." We must be faithful to keep giving to God through our tithes and offerings, and through our time and our talents.

We would be lost in this world of darkness without the light of Jesus. And because we have been blessed by that light, it is our responsibility—and it could even become our destiny—to share that light with the world. If you were stuck in a cave without batteries for a flashlight, how would you feel if your neighbor ran on ahead with his fully charged flashlight and left you in the dark? You'd wonder what in the world was wrong with him for not helping you find the way. The thing is, when we are talking about the way to our destinies and our relationship with God, the stakes are even higher. Make sure you don't miss an opportunity to share the light of Jesus with someone.

Charlie's Story
With Jesus You Are Never Lost

When I was just a small child, I used to walk with my mother to a little church around the corner from our house in downtown Raleigh. At some point I realized my father wasn't going with us, and I soon decided that if Daddy didn't have to go, then neither did I. When we moved from the downtown area, there were no churches within walking distance. Since my mom couldn't drive, she wasn't able to go any longer, but she watched church services on TV. Hearing my mother sing and pray had a great impact on me.

When I was eighteen, my father died during a heart bypass surgery. I remember walking over to the window and looking out into the sky as if trying to see into heaven and telling God that if He was the type of God who would take my father right when I really needed him, I wanted no part of this Christianity thing.

My life began to spiral out of control. I got married at twenty-one, I had a child at twenty-three, and after three years I left my wife and child, looking for something more exciting. There was a country song at the time about dying at the age of thirty that I took on as my mantra. It seemed very manly to face death so boldly, so I began speaking that over my life. The year I turned thirty I found myself not feeling quite so bold as I thought, "Sometime this year I am going to die."

Over the next few weeks and months I really started searching for answers to life after death. My wife and I had never gotten a divorce, and she agreed to give me another chance, so I moved back home. My daughter was going to church with some kids in our apartment complex by way of the church's bus, but I decided we should be in a church as a family, so I called my older brother and asked him if he would mind if we came to his church. Through a tearful, shaking voice he said he had been praying for this moment for years.

We started going every Sunday, and after a few weeks I went forward during an altar call. God's Spirit was breaking me and molding me. The next Sunday, I got baptized and made a profession of faith to be a disciple of Christ. The thoughts I had of dying when I was thirty came true, but I died to my old nature and was born a new creation in Jesus Christ.

For many years afterward life was good. I was hungry to learn Scripture and wanted to know how to share my faith with confidence. I got involved in every area of church I could, but my marriage began to suffer because I was focused more on serving others than serving my family. Then in 1989 my mother passed away. My perspective on death had changed so much that I was able to rejoice and celebrate her life instead of being angry with God for taking her. But with her death came a new season of life for me, and the damage I had done to my relationship with my wife had taken its toll. After eighteen years of marriage we divorced.

I married again after this, but we had difficulties from the beginning. In 2007 I was diagnosed with cancer and had two surgeries in six weeks to remove tumors. Because of poor choices I had made in relationships and old resentments that had come back, my life was again a mess, and I knew I needed to get a fresh start in a church where no one knew me and I could hide from all my problems. I had no idea of the journey God had planned for me, but I'd heard about a church in Clayton called C3 that was so big no one would even notice me, so I decided to give it a try.

On my first Sunday there I encountered several people when I walked in the doors who made me feel welcome, something I hadn't felt in a long time. I found a seat on the back row, just in case I needed to make a quick getaway, and made myself comfortable. But the service was very contemporary, so I decided I would leave quietly and find a more traditional church. But as I was trying to stand up, it was as though God Himself placed His hand on my shoulder and said, "Just wait. Be patient. Stay for the whole service." I sat back down even though everyone around me was still standing and singing, and I waited.

I began to shift my focus from the style of music to the words of the songs, and they began to sink into my spirit, but it was all still very unsettling for me. I was being obedient to stay, but I was still guarded. The music finally stopped. Some announcements were made, and everyone stood up to greet one another. As we sat down, Pastor Matt walked out and shouted a strange greeting, something I never thought I would hear a pastor say: "What's up, everybody?"

As Pastor Matt started preaching—better yet, explaining the Word—a calmness came over me, and I knew why God didn't want me to leave. This man has been given a gift! This was where I needed to plant myself so I could grow.

Soon I was asked to serve in some capacity. I had many friends now, and friends were what I needed. I had met a woman named Tonia, who was coming out of a divorce and not ready for a relationship, but we began to develop a friendship. After I spent some more time growing in my relationship with God, Tonia and I started dating, and now we are happily married with Christ at the center.

I look back on my life early in my Christian walk, and I can see now that I was angry with God because I felt lost. And when I did serve God, my motivation was based on fear and the need to overcome Satan's traps. Through the teachings and instruction of God's Word, I have grown in my relationship with Christ. I'm no longer lost, and fear is not a motivating factor. Love is!

Charlie spent a large part of his life feeling lost and searching for a way out. He made many wrong turns. Even when he thought he was following the light of Christ, some of his choices were actually taking him down paths that led away from God. The turning point for Charlie was when he found a place where he could connect with people who really did shine the light of Jesus into his life through their attitudes, actions, and generosity.

Are you stumbling around in the darkness the way Charlie was? What light are you using to guide your steps? How are you being a light for someone else? Can you find ways to do that more? Let Jesus be the light that helps you find your way out of difficult situations and guides your steps as you move into the future.

NEXT STEPS

Read Psalm 139:7–12:

Where shall I go from Your spirit, or where shall I flee from Your presence? If I ascend to heaven, You are there; if I make my bed in Sheol, You are there. If I take the wings of the morning and dwell at the end of the sea, even there Your hand shall guide me, and Your right hand shall take hold of me. If I say, "Surely the darkness shall cover me, and the light shall be as night about me," even the darkness is not dark to You, but the night shines as the day, for the darkness is like light to You.

—MEV

Reflect:

- What do these verses say about God's presence in your life?

- When during your life have you felt lost? How did you lose your way?

- According to these verses, what promise does God give you when you feel lost?

Declare:

Jesus, You are the light. I will overcome darkness today as I follow You.

Chapter Three

Do You Know What You Are Looking For?

I Am the Door

> I am the door. If anyone enters
> through Me, he will be saved and will
> go in and out and find pasture.
> —John 10:9, MEV

After I gave up wrestling in college, God changed the desires of my heart, and I knew He wanted me to go into ministry. I didn't know exactly what that looked like, but I knew I wanted to serve God and that probably would be with students and young adults. I saw an opportunity to join one of the school's travel teams. This particular team would go to different churches and perform music and drama for youth camps and rallies. I tried out for the team and made the first cut. I was so excited and just knew this was God's will.

My mom directed the drama ministry at our church. From the time I was in elementary school, I performed in her plays, many of which she had written herself. I also loved music and was in the All-State Choir in high school and studied music in college as well. So I just knew this was the perfect opportunity for me! It was like it was designed for me. The team had a second round of cuts, and I made it through that one. I was sure this was affirmation that I was on the right path. I was born for this job, and it was designed for me.

When they made the final round of cuts, my name was not on the list. I couldn't understand what had happened. I was sure God had gotten this wrong. I had committed to serving Him, and this was the perfect place for me to do that. How could this be? How could I not be involved in this kind of ministry? The opportunity also offered a scholarship, which would have lifted some of my financial burden. I remember feeling so confused and let down, and I really wrestled with God.

Several months later I happened to see a notice in our college newsletter for churches in the area looking for part-time youth ministers, so I went to the career office on campus and filled out the form. It was my first time putting together any kind of résumé. Nothing happened right away, and I went on about my life. Then a few months later I got a call from someone from a small country church saying it had received my application and wanted to interview me.

I ended up getting the job and spent about a year and a half there serving the youth. We started out with about fifteen kids and grew to forty-five to fifty in a congregation of about 105. It was an amazing place to grow and learn and prepare myself for the things I would be called to do later in ministry. I look back now and see how God was working in me and preparing me. I served in student ministry for thirteen years, and then God called my wife and me to help start C3 Church.

I realized later that if I had pushed my way through that first door I thought was the right one, I never would have been available to walk through the door that led to the blessings and direction for my life that God had planned all along. I wouldn't be where I am today if I had tried to force open the wrong door or had lived with a bitter attitude.

A lot of times when God is trying to lead us one way, we want to go another and end up opening a lot of doors that take us in the wrong direction. One of the toughest choices we face in life is deciding what we are looking for from life. Figuring that out is often tied to deciding whether we are going to look for our own doors or look to God to lead us.

Do You Know What You're Searching For?

Many people spend their whole lives looking for a door that will lead them to happiness and fulfillment. Often something we experienced in childhood can carry into our adult life and cause us to keep walking through every door possible to find hope.

If we look to God, we will find that Jesus is the door

that opens up to all the amazing things God has planned for us here on earth and that wait for us in heaven.

Selecting the Right Doors

When I was a kid I used to watch the game show *Let's Make a Deal*. Contestants are presented with opportunities to trade something they have for an unknown item in a box behind a curtain. They progress through the game until they are presented with the option of choosing what's behind door number 1, door number 2, or door number 3. One door might lead to an all-expenses-paid vacation or a new car. The next might offer some small kitchen appliance or a year's supply of laundry detergent. The last door might be hiding a billy goat or a broken-down junk car, and the contestant would get "zonked."

It was always exciting to watch as the audience shouted out which door the contestants should pick. They were guessing, but their choice of door was based on where they thought the best opportunity lay. You probably don't have a live studio audience around to help you decide what door to choose in life, and it can be really intimidating to make a choice when you don't know what you might end up with.

Sometimes we go on our gut instinct, guessing what might be behind a door, and sometimes we choose based on what a door looks like from the outside. Some doors are elaborately carved and decorated, like the ones on cathedrals and state buildings. Some stand out because of their size, and others are appealing because they are hard to locate or open. Then there are doors that have a lot of symbolic significance.

Regardless of what these doors look like on the outside, most of the time what makes them significant is what lies behind them. Choosing the right door can make all the difference in how our lives unfold from the moment we step through it.

Sometimes we will encounter a door where what lies on the other side is not something we want to be associated with, such as a jail cell or a reprimand from the human resources department. Or the door may lead to bad news we wish we could avoid, such as a negative doctor's report or a bad meeting with your child's principal.

Then there are the doors that open up to good things, such as a big surprise party or the pizza delivery guy. Most people enjoy going outdoors into the warm sun in the summer or coming indoors away from the cold in the winter. And probably one of the best doors is the one to our home, where we find a family member or pet waiting eagerly for our arrival. It can be hard to tell by how things look on the outside whether you will encounter a blessing or a trial when you walk through a door, so it is important to learn how to choose the right ones to open.

It's just a fact of life that we aren't able to see into the future to know where our choices are going to lead us, though some might seem pretty obvious. But we do have an incredible guide for choosing the right doors if we just pay attention.

Closing Old Doors and Opening New Ones

If I'd had my way back in college, I would have gone through the wrong door because I was looking for the wrong thing. Actually, I may have been looking for the right thing but for the wrong reasons. And that is another aspect of answering the question "What are you looking for?"

When we are seeking God and allowing His Word to guide us, we can avoid some of the bad outcomes by letting God direct us—not just the choices we make for our lives, but where our hearts and minds are as we make those decisions. But even when we end up in trouble or faced with a problem, He can get us back on track if we let Him.

James 1:2 says, "Dear brothers and sisters, when troubles of any kind come your way, consider it an opportunity for great joy." We are going to face challenges in life, but those problems and troubles can become doors of opportunity! Facing a problem is an opportunity for great joy—an opportunity for us to grow in our faith! It is important that we realize that in order to discern God's will for our lives.

> **Dear brothers and sisters, when troubles of any kind come your way, consider it an opportunity for great joy. —James 1:2**

James says to count it all joy when we experience trials and temptations because when we let God direct us, He can make something beautiful out of our struggles. We don't have to settle for the imitation blessings with which the devil tries to tempt us. When we open the door God has for us, He can turn our troubles into triumphs. He can turn our mess into a message. He can turn our pain into a purpose. Every problem is an opportunity for God to do something new and exciting because in the way God works, when one door closes, another door opens.

Let's look at some doors God can open when we are facing trials.

DOORS OF FREEDOM

Freedom is one of the most powerful doors we can walk through—and it is a door many people never truly experience. I've learned that we can begin a relationship with God immediately, but discovering freedom is a process.

Many people live their whole lives never truly experiencing freedom from their past. God doesn't want us to live forever with regret from past addictions, sin, or abuse. He wants to set us free. Jesus came to save us and set us free. Salvation happens immediately after we accept Him in our hearts as Savior and Lord, but freedom is a journey. Experiencing true freedom is like peeling an onion one layer at a time.

Not too long ago the Holy Spirit reminded me of something that happened to me that I had completely buried without realizing it. When I was in high school, a good friend invited me over to his home and attempted to make sexual advances toward me. I had dismissed it because I was able to fight him off. But after that I tried to prove my manhood and lost my virginity to someone I didn't even know. I hurt people because I was wounded.

Although I have experienced freedom in so many ways since I was saved, this is one thing I carried with me until recently. And it was a men's small group that provided a safe place for me to share my story and to experience authentic healing. I've discovered that healing comes when we are honest with safe, trustworthy people about what is happening in our lives. James 5:16 says, "Confess your sins to each other and pray for each other so that you may be healed. The earnest prayer of a righteous person has great power and produces wonderful results."

The following Bible story about Peter shows us how God can lead us to the doors of escape or lead us out of negative situations in which we find ourselves. It is one of the most powerful illustrations of God's taking a troubling situation and literally flinging a door of opportunity open to provide freedom:

> The night before Peter was to be placed on trial, he was asleep, fastened with two chains between two soldiers. Others stood guard at the prison gate. Suddenly, there was a bright light in the cell, and an angel of the Lord stood before Peter. The angel struck him on the side to awaken him and said, "Quick! Get up!" And the chains fell off his wrists. Then the angel told him, "Get dressed and put on your sandals." And he did. "Now put on your coat and follow me," the angel ordered.
>
> —ACTS 12:6–8

Peter's situation looked hopeless, but in those darkest moments God turned his trial into an opportunity and set

Peter free from his oppressors. But there is something else to notice in this story:

> So Peter left the cell, following the angel. But all the time he thought it was a vision. He didn't realize it was actually happening. They passed the first and second guard posts and came to the iron gate leading to the city, and this opened for them all by itself. So they passed through and started walking down the street, and then the angel suddenly left him.
>
> Peter finally came to his senses. "It's really true!" he said. "The Lord has sent his angel and saved me from Herod and from what the Jewish leaders had planned to do to me!"
>
> When he realized this, he went to the home of Mary, the mother of John Mark, where many were gathered for prayer. He knocked at the door in the gate, and a servant girl named Rhoda came to open it. When she recognized Peter's voice, she was so overjoyed that, instead of opening the door, she ran back inside and told everyone, "Peter is standing at the door!"
>
> "You're out of your mind!" they said. When she insisted, they decided, "It must be his angel."
>
> Meanwhile, Peter continued knocking. When they finally opened the door and saw him, they were amazed. He motioned for them to quiet down and told them how the Lord had led him out of prison. "Tell James and the other brothers

what happened," he said. And then he went to another place.

—Acts 12:9–17

Peter didn't just ride off into the sunset celebrating his good fortune. He made sure to go and tell people about what God had done for him. This became an opportunity for him to praise God.

We can have freedom in Jesus, and His truth will set us free. But it is important to make sure we never miss an opportunity to praise Him and share with others the freedom He offers.

Doors of Service

My nephew Owen lives in Houston, Texas, and always dreamed of playing basketball in the NBA. He and his dad, Rod, love to watch college and NBA games, as well as the NBA Draft. During the NBA Draft in the summer of 2014 an All-American player named Isaiah Austin from Baylor University was projected to be drafted in the first round and make millions of dollars, fulfilling his own life-long dream of playing in the NBA. However, Isaiah could not be drafted because just a few days earlier he had been diagnosed with a rare, life-threatening disorder called Marfan syndrome.

During the draft there was a lot of news coverage on ESPN and other media outlets about Isaiah's new diagnosis, which ended his professional basketball career before it even started. Owen's father, my brother-in-law Rod, began to recognize in Owen the symptoms of Marfan syndrome. As a result Rod took Owen to the doctor to get tested the next day.

As it turned out, Owen had the same disorder as Isaiah did, shattering his dream of playing NBA basketball. He was told he could not play the game he so loved ever again because his heart and body could not take the rigorous demands basketball brings.

When Owen heard the devastating news of his diagnosis, he cried for a few moments and then told his dad he was still very young and could still become a coach or a referee, or have some other type of job in the NBA. And even though he had Marfan syndrome, he could still live a long life. He also said he wanted to take something bad in his life and make it good. He wanted to help others.

Sometime later I asked Owen how he was dealing with this big change in his life, and I will never forget what he told me. He said, "I decided I can either make it my excuse or my purpose. So I am going to make it my purpose." From the day of his diagnosis Owen got involved with the Isaiah Austin Foundation to support Isaiah's efforts to raise money for and awareness of Marfan syndrome.

I decided I can either make it my excuse or my purpose. So I am going to make it my purpose.
—Owen Gray

Owen has personally raised over $50,000 for Isaiah's organization. He and Isaiah are now like brothers as a result of their diagnosis, and they have changed so many lives. Owen has also become deeply involved with the Marfan Foundation (www.marfan.org)

and has raised more than $150,000 for Marfan syndrome research, education, and awareness. He and Isaiah have lobbied senators and congressmen in Washington, DC, and regularly speak all over the country, educating people about Marfan syndrome and related disorders and providing hope for those who suffer the effects of Marfan.

Owen has even been featured on ESPN. He has received awards and recognition from former president Barack Obama, senators, congressmen, and the Houston Rockets, and the National Home School Basketball Association has even named an annual award after him. It's called the Owen Gray Heart of a Champion Award. In just two years God has opened all kinds of doors for Owen to serve Him and positively impact the lives of so many people. Those are opportunities he may never have had if he had allowed disappointment to keep him from God's purpose for his life.

Maybe you have a heart for service too but are trying to dictate to God when, where, and how that service should take place. That's not necessarily a bad thing because any desire to share the gospel comes from God, but it really restricts the potential for how lives can be changed if you don't let God have free reign in your life. We, in our humanness, are pretty short-sighted and don't have the ability to imagine all that could be done through God's handiwork. When we allow Him

> **And pray for us, too, that God may open a door for our message, so that we may proclaim the mystery of Christ, for which I am in chains.**
> **—Colossians 4:3, NIV**

to guide our steps, we are led to the doors that the people we are supposed to serve are waiting behind.

DOORS OF SACRIFICE

My inability to see God working in my life as I was looking for a ministry opportunity in college caused me to waste a lot of time being resentful and questioning whether God knew what He was doing. I didn't want to give up on my version of the dream because I thought I had my life planned out perfectly. I had some pride that God needed to get out of me. I had to figure out how to sacrifice my own desires and expectations so God could show me the plan He actually did have for me. I had to lay down my need to control the situation and surrender to God's ability to take me even further than I imagined. That was not easy because it meant sacrificing my pride to do something that, in my limited understanding, seemed smaller and didn't offer as much glamour and attention.

So you're probably not thinking, "Yay, Matt! Sacrifice! Just what I always wanted!" In fact, what's running through your head probably sounds more like, "Wait, Matt! Sacrifice is not at all what I had in mind! That's a door I definitely don't want to open!"

The thing is God blesses us when we endure trials and temptations! This is the realization we come to when we totally get it—when we finally understand that our lives are all about Jesus. When you are willing to do whatever, go wherever, give whatever, say whatever, and your prayer is, "Not my will but Your will be done," you are opening a door to receive great blessings from God because you are opening the door of your heart to Him. We become kingdom builders and world changers because we have surrendered everything we have and everything we are to Jesus.

Doors of Grace

One of the really cool parts of C. S. Lewis's *The Lion, the Witch, and the Wardrobe* is when Lucy goes into Narnia, and all kinds of crazy things happen, and she can spend long periods there when only a few seconds have passed back in the "real" world. She opens a door and goes into a world of wild adventures, some not turning out so well, and all of that goes away as soon as she steps back through the wardrobe and into the bedroom where her family is.

How many times in your life have you wanted to be able to undo things that have happened? To be able to turn around, go back to where you started, and have a do-over? Can you imagine how great it would be to walk back through a door you opened by mistake or out of foolish-

> **Continue to ask, and God will give to you. Continue to search, and you will find. Continue to knock, and the door will open for you.**
> **—Matthew 7:7, ERV**

ness, a door that led you to a situation that turned out badly or not as you had hoped?

The door of grace offers us one of the greatest opportunities we could hope for. After all of the wrong doors we have opened that have led us down wrong paths and into troublesome experiences, we need grace more than anything else. Knowing Jesus isn't going to magically make us stop choosing poorly. We are human and will make mistakes and selfish choices, and fail to see the bigger picture. That is why we need Jesus in the first place! Through His guidance we can learn to avoid some of these wrong doors. And when all else fails, His grace and forgiveness allow us to have a fresh start!

Doors of Opportunity

As we go through life, we will come across many doors of opportunity, but not all of them are doors we are meant to go through. That can be tough to discern and even harder to accept because we have a tendency to want to investigate every opportunity on the off chance that it might lead us to something that is *big*, a game changer. The problem is that not everything that comes our way is right for us to pursue.

It is a lot easier to identify and avoid the bad ideas, even though we sometimes still choose them—such as the time I left my mic on when I ran to the bathroom before a sermon. The sound guys really had to scramble to mute it and unfortunately weren't quite quick enough! If I had just taken it off instead of trying to save myself a little hassle, I wouldn't have embarrassed myself.

But those types of choices are a little easier to identify. The challenge comes when we are presented with an opportunity that isn't illegal, dangerous, unhealthy, or socially unacceptable and looks good on the surface. Those choices are a lot more difficult because there may not be anything overtly wrong with them; they just don't get us closer to God's plan for our lives. They might be detours that delay our accomplishing things God has planned for us, or they might have long-term consequences we can't see from our limited perspective.

These may be *good* opportunities, but it doesn't mean they are *God* opportunities. That is an important distinction and one we have to learn to discern if we are going to avoid opening the wrong doors and spending time on the wrong pursuits. If I had been able to join the Touring Team in college, it would have been a good opportunity for me and would have been a lot of fun. I probably could have done a lot of really good things with it. But it wasn't a God opportunity because He had a different path in mind to prepare me for a larger role down the road.

I can't take credit for making the right choice in that situation because it was made for me. But this story is a

Is it a *good* opportunity, or a *God* opportunity?

good illustration of how some opportunities look good from our perspective, and there are no obvious reasons to avoid them, yet there are things we don't know that make them the wrong way to go.

Our third "I am" declaration comes from John 10:9–10: "*I am the door.* If anyone enters through Me, he will be saved and will go in and out and find pasture.... I came that they may have life, and that they may have it more abundantly" (MEV, emphasis added).

We will encounter many situations in life that seem good, such as they might be the doors Jesus is opening for us. So how do we know what to pursue and what to pass up? Here are three questions you can ask yourself for some guidance:

1. Have I really taken this to God in prayer and listened for Him to answer?

2. Am I interested in this opportunity because it brings glory to me, or because it will bring glory to God?

3. If I pass on this opportunity, can I still serve God in other ways?

The most important thing is to take the time to prayerfully consider your choice before you make a move to ensure God is leading you. No matter what you are looking for behind the doors you open, the most important thing you should hope to find is Jesus there waiting to lead you to your purpose and to God's will for your life.

But wait, there is one more door that I want to share with you. And this is by far the best door of all: the door to our hearts. The Bible tells us that Jesus is at the door waiting for us: "Look! I stand at the door and knock. If you hear my voice and open the door, I will come in, and we will share a meal together as friends" (Rev. 3:20).

We are going to open a lot of doors in our lifetimes, and we will pass by many more that we don't open for whatever reason. But no matter what we are hoping to find on the other side of the doors we open, there really is only one door that matters—the one that leads us to

Jesus. Jesus is the only door to salvation—the only one. But the cool thing is that door does not restrict access. And after we go through that door, we become identified with what is on the other side.

Jill's Story
Jesus Is the Answer

My husband, Mark, and I moved to Clayton, North Carolina, in 2004 from Miami, Florida. We had already found C3 online, and Mark had visited before we came up. It felt like home as soon as we walked into the lobby. We didn't know anybody but soon got involved in a connect group, and it didn't take long for us to make friends.

At C3 we've been encouraged and equipped to grow as leaders, and we led connect groups for years and then became coaches to the leaders. It's always amazing to see how God works in each of the groups. As part of our connect group one year we had a "baby shower" for a new ministry in town. As part of the shower the director showed us videos describing the many facets of a Christian pregnancy center, and I found myself identifying with a woman who described her experience of finding healing from a past abortion.

I got up afterward and told my group my

abortion story and felt God was leading me to volunteer at the center. I have been involved with this ministry for more than eight years now and am the director of the Restoration Ministry—part of iChoose Pregnancy and Support Services—where I lead and oversee Bible studies for post-abortive women. I'm so glad I had the courage to tell my secret to that group when I felt God opening that door. As I have continued to be mentored by my leaders at C3, God has given me many opportunities to overcome my past and my mistakes to help others find freedom.

At C3 we have always been taught the value of serving others, so my family has been involved in ministry teams and has served in many different areas through the years. Another area I've been involved in for several years is our special needs classrooms. God called me to serve, and I've been amazed how He keeps growing my capacity to help these children and their families.

When I started at C3 those many years ago, I was a head-knowledge Christian and set in my ways. But because of the doors that have been opened through sermons, connect groups, trainings, and opportunities to serve, my life is being transformed. I have experienced life change and God's forgiveness and mercy so I can help others do the same. I am not the person I was. I am a better worshipper, wife, parent, friend, and leader.

This is a burning question for sure: What am I looking for? And it's one we might go our entire lives trying to answer. Jill had made a lot of poor choices for her life, and she not only needed God's grace and freedom from her past sin and pain, but she also needed the gift of service. Choosing to serve opened her up to the God opportunities that would ultimately bring the healing she needed.

The only way to really get beyond the surface of what we are looking for, where we aren't just addressing immediate physical needs, is to turn to God. We have to trust Him to guide us to the doors of opportunity that will lead us where He wants us to go. We have to be willing to give up our own agendas and our own expectations so He can reveal to us what He put us here to accomplish and touch the lives of those we are intended to reach.

Are you facing some difficult decisions in your life right now? If so, have you opened the door of your heart and invited Jesus in? If not, I encourage you to do so. Let Him help you determine whether the choice before you is a *good* opportunity or a *God* opportunity and decide which door to open.

NEXT STEPS

Read Romans 10:9–13:

If you declare with your mouth, "Jesus is Lord," and believe in your heart that God raised him from the dead, you will be saved. For it is with your heart that you believe and are justified, and it is with your mouth that you profess your faith and are saved. As Scripture says, "Anyone who believes in him will never be put to shame." For there is no difference between Jew and Gentile— the same Lord is Lord of all and richly blesses all who call on him, for, "Everyone who calls on the name of the Lord will be saved."

—NIV

Reflect:

- What do these verses say you must do to be saved?

- If you have never called upon the name of the Lord to be saved, then pray something like this:

Dear God, thank You for sending Your only Son to die on the cross and rise from the grave. I repent of my sins and ask You to come into my heart and be my Savior and Lord. I declare with my mouth that Jesus is Lord and believe in my heart that You were raised from the grave.

Thank You for saving me. Help me live for You the rest of my life. In Jesus's name, amen.

Declare:

I declare that Jesus Christ is my Lord and Savior, and I will live for Him. God has a perfect plan and purpose for my life, and He will open the doors that I am to walk through.

Chapter Four

Do You Know Whom You Can Trust?

I Am the Good Shepherd

I am the good shepherd. The good
shepherd sacrifices his life for the sheep.
—John 10:11

I USED TO THINK when I was younger, "I bet it would be awesome to be a pastor because everyone in church just loves one another, and it must be so peaceful all the time." Then I became a lead pastor, and I soon learned that leading a congregation is not easy. Being a pastor is awesome, but when you are dealing with people who are hurting, sometimes they hurt others, including their leaders.

When Martha and I helped start C3 Church in 1998, our church saw rapid growth nearly from the beginning, even though we were meeting in an elementary school cafeteria and I had never been a senior pastor before. People's lives were being changed, and they were bringing their friends. Earlier I described what some people call the miracle on an old tobacco field, where we were blessed with property to build a facility just three and a half years into our life as a church.

It really seemed God was paving the way for our church to do amazing things in the community and that the congregation was united in the common goal of serving Clayton in Jesus's name. But in the months leading up to getting in our building, something happened that I wasn't expecting. A handful of people started talking negatively, and often it was about me. I'm not sure what was said, but I know they weren't happy. I had prayed with some of these people during times of need and even baptized them. So when they started saying things about the church and about me behind my back, initially I was heartbroken by the betrayal. I was blindsided!

Even though the church continued to grow, we saw approximately one hundred people leave the church just before we occupied our new building. After we celebrated and dedicated our new building in March of 2002, I wanted to quit, as I was becoming convinced that I had taken the church as far as I could. I told myself I was not cut out to be a senior pastor and someone else needed to take the church to its next level.

I wasn't trying to quit on God. I didn't even want to quit ministry. I just wanted to quit being a senior pastor.

I thought everyone would be better off if I went back to being a student minister or even an associate pastor. It didn't help any that during that time a job opportunity came up that I wasn't even looking for.

I shared my concerns with my leadership team, and they told me to take a break, spend some time in prayer, and see how I felt in a few days. So I took a three-day sabbatical to Charleston, South Carolina. (That's about all you can afford when you are a church planter!) I had contacted Pastor Greg Surratt's office about my spending some time with him. Greg is the founding pastor of Seacoast Church, a thriving congregation in Charleston. He barely knew who I was, but he took time to hang out with me. At that time Greg golfed every Monday, so his assistant said if I wanted to spend time with Greg, I needed to golf.

Obviously I agreed to go with him even though I had been golfing only about two times in my life. I am a pretty good athlete, but I was horrible at golfing that day! The phrase I kept hearing Greg say was, "Well, that shot wasn't too bad." That was about as good as it got. I probably could have done better, but in my mind I was putting the name of someone who had hurt me on each ball, so I was subconsciously trying to destroy the ball with all my might, not just hit it.

Later that day Greg and I sat in a coffee shop while I shared with him all that had happened. Even though the church was doing great, I wasn't doing very well. I told him I wanted to quit being a pastor. Greg patiently listened to me, and then he said, "Matt, people come, and people go.

It's part of building and growing a church. Not everyone is going to stay with you forever."

I shared more of my hurts and disappointments, and he repeated that same observation over and over. He said something like, "Matt, people have gotten mad at me and left the church. It's part of the deal." It wasn't really any kind of earth-shattering revelation or deep philosophical insight. He just let me know I wasn't alone and offered me the encouragement I needed to keep going.

That conversation with Greg led to a relationship that has continued to this day, and through Greg I have met literally hundreds of pastors, many of whom have become great friends. Later, when a church-planting organization called the Association of Related Churches (ARC) was formed, Greg and I began working together to help other pastors and church planters overcome some of the same challenges we have faced and to plant life-giving churches across the United States and beyond.

Looking back now, I am so thankful I didn't give up just because a few people disappointed me. It definitely is not the only time I've been hurt in ministry, but through it I have learned to trust God and lean on others. God didn't create us to do life alone; we need one another to live the life of purpose He has planned for us.

HAVE YOU EVER BEEN LET DOWN?

Are you feeling wounded and betrayed? Have you ever put your trust in someone who ended up letting you down? Maybe you put your trust in your husband or wife, and your spouse left you. Perhaps you put your trust in a business partner, and he embezzled from the company. Maybe you put your trust in a teacher or coach, and that person hurt or abused you. These can be devastating experiences that can impact the rest of your life. The good news is that Jesus says He will never leave us or forsake us! Though people may let us down, God will never fail us! He will prove to us over and over how He is right beside us to protect us from harm.

JESUS IS THE GOOD SHEPHERD

The Bible often refers to Jesus as a shepherd and to us as His flock. Let's talk about what that means for us. We don't run across a whole lot of shepherds here in the United States these days. In fact, I bet most people have never even been close to a sheep. In the part of the world where Jesus lived, it was common to encounter a shepherd and his sheep.

In the Middle East, where Jesus lived, sheep were kept in sheepfolds, which were low, ring-shaped stone walls with an opening a couple of feet wide. They were quite different from the corrals you might see here. And you might be surprised to learn the sheepfold didn't have a gate or door across the opening.

You're probably thinking, "How in the world was that secure?" Well, on its own it wouldn't have been, but the shepherd served as the door to the sheepfold. He stood guard there during the day, and he slept across the threshold at night, making sure the sheep stayed where they were supposed to be and the thieves and wild beasts kept away from his precious flock.

This is what Jesus was trying to explain to the Pharisees in John 10 about who He was—and who He is to us. He is our protector, putting Himself between us and those who want to harm us. He is also standing guard over us to keep us from wandering away from safety.

In this description of Jesus as the Good Shepherd we find our fourth "I am" declaration:

> *I am the good shepherd.* The good shepherd sacrifices his life for the sheep. A hired hand will run when he sees a wolf coming. He will abandon the sheep because they don't belong to him and he isn't their shepherd. And so the wolf attacks them and scatters the flock. The hired hand runs away because he's working only for the money and doesn't really care about the sheep. I am the good shepherd; I know my own sheep, and they know me, just as my Father knows me and I know the Father. So I sacrifice my life for the sheep. I have other sheep, too, that are not in this sheepfold. I must bring them also. They will listen to my voice, and there will be one flock with one shepherd.
>
> —JOHN 10:11–16, EMPHASIS ADDED

In these verses Jesus lists two specific things the Good Shepherd does: 1) He sacrifices Himself for His sheep to protect them from attacks, and 2) He knows His sheep—how many there are, what they need, and when they have wandered away.

The Good Shepherd Sacrifices Himself for His Sheep

When we understand how a shepherd lies across the door to protect his sheep, we get a really vivid picture of the way Jesus works in our lives to keep us from harm. In the Old Testament the Israelites used an altar to offer sacrifices for the forgiveness of their sins. When Jesus came to earth, He sacrificed His life on the cross as the perfect and complete sacrifice! He is our sacrificial Lamb.

The Bible says, "So let us come boldly to the throne of our gracious God. There we will receive his mercy, and we will find grace to help us when we need it most" (Heb. 4:16). All we need to do is come to Jesus, and He will provide the grace and mercy we need!

Most adults can vividly remember where they were and what they were doing on September 11, 2001. They have a 9/11 story. Some of us may even have it burned in our memories more than a wedding day, a graduation, or the birth of a child. I definitely remember where I was. Actually, I was in the air at the time, flying to Nashville, Tennessee, at the same time the planes were hitting the World Trade Center towers.

> So let us come boldly to the throne of our gracious God. There we will receive his mercy, and we will find grace to help us when we need it most.
> —Hebrews 4:16

I was traveling with another minister to visit a pastor friend for a few days, and a member of the church staff picked us up from the airport. While we were in the car, the man's wife called him, and I could tell from his response that something was wrong. After he got off the phone, he told us that there were reports of a plane flying into a building in New York City.

When we arrived at the church, they had the news on. We started seeing reports about the Pentagon also being attacked and other details rolling in that made me feel as if this truly was the end of the world. I fell to my knees in prayer, as it seemed our world was crumbling around us.

Recording artist Michael W. Smith called the pastor about hosting a prayer and worship gathering that night. He pulled together some of the most well-known artists in Christian music, and we spent the evening praying and praising God. As I prayed, I realized that my security was not to be found in our government or our military. It wasn't going to come from my bank account or the things of this world. It wasn't in how popular or celebrated I could become. My security is in God; He is the One who protects and guides me. He is the only One I truly trust to never leave or forsake me.

We have this tendency to get lost and wander into trouble, a lot like sheep do. Being saved means being guarded by Jesus and being shepherded in the way we act, where we go, and how we choose to live. It may not be the most flattering thing to be called sheep, but in reality we act that way more than we want to admit. I know I have found myself off course more than once without realizing I was headed there.

We have a Savior who lived a sacrificial life for us and ultimately gave His *life* for us on the cross. He was our sacrificial Lamb! Now God is calling us to be shepherds for others. He has called us to reach out to other lost sheep.

The Good Shepherd Knows His Sheep

The realization I had after 9/11 about where my comfort and security come from was important not just because it helped me feel safer in a world that was all of a sudden a lot more dangerous, but because it reassured me that God is looking out for me and is the source of my strength and my peace.

As we read earlier, Jesus is clear about the lengths He will go to in order to protect us: He laid down His life for us! In John 10:14–15 He says, "I am the good shepherd; I know my sheep and my sheep know me—just as the Father knows me and I know the Father—and I lay down my life for the sheep" (NIV).

But He's also pretty clear about the fact that you have to be in the fold for Him to be able to do that. Being in the fold means you know Him and have a relationship with Him. He isn't trying to leave you out in the cold. He wants you to be with Him. He says in John 10:16, "I have other sheep who are not of this fold. I must also bring them, and they will hear [or listen to] My voice. There will be one flock and one shepherd" (MEV). Jesus is reaching out to all of us, trying to bring us in and keep us close to Him.

This means there is security in having Jesus identify you as His! When we have our identity in Him, He represents us to the Father, and He looks after us the way a shepherd tends his flock. In a time when there is so much to make us feel insecure, isn't it a relief to know there is a place that offers us relief from that feeling?

Whether you are one of the lost sheep or know someone who is, it is important to understand just what it means to be identified by God as His and to find our identity in Him.

In 1 Peter 2:25 the Bible tells us, "Once you were like sheep who wandered away. But now you have turned to your Shepherd, the Guardian of your souls." He knows exactly what we need. He rejoices when we have happiness in our lives, and His heart breaks when we experience sorrow. The Bible tells us He has counted all the hairs on our heads and knows our hearts' deepest desires.

He cares about every one of us! In fact, He cares about every *single* one of us on an individual and personal level. This story from the Bible illustrates how important each of us is to God:

> So Jesus told them this story: "If a man has a hundred sheep and one of them gets lost, what will he do? Won't he leave the ninety-nine others in the wilderness and go to search for the one that is lost until he finds it? And when he has found it, he will joyfully carry it home on his shoulders. When he arrives, he will call together his friends and neighbors, saying, 'Rejoice with me because I have found my lost sheep.' In the same way, there is more joy in heaven over one lost sinner who repents and returns to God than over ninety-nine others who are righteous and haven't strayed away!"
> —Luke 15:3–7

This passage of Scripture shows me that every person matters to God. Many people have this view of God—that He's mad at us or He is out to make our lives miserable. But it is actually the opposite. He sacrificed Himself to make sure that each of us has a good life and will be with Him in heaven afterward. And He is not willing to leave any of us behind.

He is a good God—the good Shepherd tending to His sheep. He loves you, cares about you, and wants to bless you. Psalm 23 is one of my favorite chapters in the Bible. Often when I feel overwhelmed and restless, I just start quoting Psalm 23. If I am having a hard time going to sleep because my mind is racing, I can recite this passage of Scripture in my mind, and a peace comes over me that assures me that the Lord is my Shepherd and I have all I need!

> **Rejoice with me because I have found my lost sheep.**
> **–Luke 15:6**

> The LORD is my shepherd; I have all that I need.
> He lets me rest in green meadows; he leads me
>   beside peaceful streams.
> He renews my strength. He guides me along right
>   paths, bringing honor to his name.
> Even when I walk through the darkest valley, I will
>   not be afraid, for you are close beside me.
> Your rod and your staff protect and comfort me.
> You prepare a feast for me in the presence of my
>   enemies.
> You honor me by anointing my head with oil.
>   My cup overflows with blessings.

> Surely your goodness and unfailing love will pursue
> me all the days of my life, and I will live in
> the house of the Lord forever.
>
> —Psalm 23

This is what it means to be saved by the Good Shepherd. He looks after our every need, from the basics of food, water, and shelter to the restorative aspects of rest, peace, and comfort. He makes us feel safe in this life, and He ensures our eternal security as well.

In Luke 12:22–24 Jesus tells us in even plainer terms how important we are to God:

> That is why I tell you not to worry about everyday life—whether you have enough food to eat or enough clothes to wear. For life is more than food, and your body more than clothing. Look at the ravens. They don't plant or harvest or store food in barns, for God feeds them. And you are far more valuable to him than any birds!

God is good to us. He always will be good to us. And if you trust Him to guide you, He will make sure your needs are met.

Amanda's Story
You Can Always Trust God

When "life" brought Tom and me together, I was a young woman, nervous about what was next for me in life with a nine-month-old child from a previous relationship, living with my mom, and partying when I could. I didn't really have a church life. I went maybe twice a year on the holidays and prayed when life was hard. Tom, on the other hand, seemed to have his life together—a good job, a good income, and living the young man's single life.

Eventually things got more serious between us, and we talked of marriage and a future. One day my mom's neighbor spotted Tom outside in the yard and invited him to visit C3 Church. When he asked me to go, I thought, "Maybe, but I just want to have fun and sleep in after late Saturday nights out." But we ended up going, and in the months that followed we continued to attend even though some mornings, I

> **And my God will meet all your needs according to the riches of his glory in Christ Jesus.**
> **–Philippians 4:19, NIV**

hate to admit, it was while hungover. But we were getting something valuable in those days that I wasn't aware of at the time. Now I know hearing the message of Jesus allowed us to build our foundation as a couple to take on the situations in our future that would have torn us apart.

Tom is a very firm believer in tithing, and we began doing that. As we did, we were blessed in our business, and it grew. Even in hard times we stayed faithful and continued to give, even when we thought we'd lose it all. God blessed us, and we never lost.

After we were married and ready to add to the family, we began trying to get pregnant. After a year and a half of no success, I went to the doctor and found out I had polycystic ovarian syndrome, which meant it would be difficult for me to get pregnant. Devastated is exactly what we were. We asked, "Why? Why us?"

After the shock wore off and the dust settled, we decided to do the twenty-one-day Daniel fast the church does every year. We thought we'd pray and fast and see what happened. I had been trying everything, including things such as holistic medicine, desperately searching for answers. After completing the fast and attending church one Wednesday night, my heart was just taken by the Holy Spirit. The band played the most beautiful song I'd ever heard, called "Healer." The song says that nothing is impossible for God. I nearly hit the floor in a puddle of tears. It spoke to my heart and reassured me that God had everything in His hands.

A few months later we took a pregnancy test that was positive! In that moment I declared Jesus was my healer! It wasn't long before our healthy baby girl arrived. And then five years after that we had a healthy little boy.

Tom and I have had issues with money, trust, and just life in general, but God has shown up. Sometimes it seems He is there early, and sometimes it seems to be just in the nick of time. We like to say He comes at 11:59:59, meaning just before things fall apart.

C3 has been our wake-up call from day one. We have learned that God is and always will be faithful. As we continue to stay with Him, no matter how good or bad our days are, we know we can trust that His plan is better than ours. Today we are stronger. As storms linger, we press in to His Word and proclaim, "God's got this!"

Amanda faced some big struggles in her faith early on and began to wonder if she could trust God. By staying in His Word and praying, she found out not only that she could trust Him but also that He had even greater plans for her than she could have imagined.

Have you ever shared something personal with a friend in confidence, only to find out the person went and told other people? Have you ever relied on someone to do something, and she dropped the ball? Has someone ever attacked you with his words, and you barely even knew who he was? If you live long enough, I imagine all these and more can happen to you. But you don't have to continue feeling alone and hopeless. Jesus will always be there, and He will always come through, even if it doesn't fit the timing you want. His timing is always better.

Here are some things I've learned about trusting God through hard times:

- Reach out to someone for help. Find someone who is perhaps older and has wisdom from God, and just share with that person what you are going through.

- Don't do life alone. God didn't create us to do life alone. We need one another! The Bible says, "Two are better than one, because they have a good return for their labor: if either of them falls down, one can help the other up. But pity anyone who falls and has no one to help them up" (Eccles. 4:9–10, NIV).

- Decide that you aren't going to quit. Other people are counting on you! You have influence, and we need you to stay in the race! Aren't you thankful that God didn't give up on you?

- Remember that you can trust God. He is your Good Shepherd! In fact, when we put our total trust in Him, we live with the security that He is our Good Shepherd, so when others hurt us, it doesn't have as much impact.

NEXT STEPS

Read Psalm 23:

The LORD is my shepherd, I lack nothing. He makes me lie down in green pastures, he leads me beside quiet waters, he refreshes my soul. He guides me along the right paths for his name's sake. Even though I walk through the darkest valley, I will fear no evil, for you are with me; your rod and your staff, they comfort me. You prepare a table before me in the presence of my enemies. You anoint my head with oil; my cup overflows. Surely your goodness and love will follow me all the days of my life, and I will dwell in the house of the LORD forever.

—NIV

Reflect:

- List all the things this passage says God does for us.

- Have you trusted God to be all these things for you?

- Where do you feel you put your trust when you are not fully trusting God?

Declare:

God, You are my Shepherd, my guide, my protector, my banner of victory. You are everything I need. You are I Am.

Chapter Five

Do You Need Power?

I Am the Resurrection and the Life

I am the resurrection and the life. Anyone
who believes in me will live, even after dying.
—JOHN 11:25

𝒩EW OPPORTUNITIES CAN create new challenges. Even
when we experience good things, we often need to make
adjustments. For example, if you get a new car, you have to
get adjusted to where all the controls are. If you get a new
smartphone or new upgrades, you may have to watch a tuto-
rial to learn how to access all the new features.

Big and small opportunities alike can put us in a position of transition and adjustment. For example, several
years ago after Martha and I moved to Virginia, we were
blessed to purchase a new home. Although it was small, we

were so excited to have a new house where we could watch our two girls grow (our son Caleb came later). Family and friends helped us unload boxes and furniture from the truck. Martha and I worked quickly to get the boxes unpacked so we could get settled in.

Anytime you move into a new home, some things are different from what you are used to. Martha was determined to make sure we unpacked boxes as quickly as possible, but our first priority (at least as far as I was concerned) was to get the TV set up so I could watch the college football bowl games. I got the television and cable box out and plugged them in, sat down, and pushed the appropriate buttons on the remote. Nothing happened. I shook the remote. I took the batteries out and put them back in. I tried again, and the light on the remote lit up, but the TV wouldn't come on.

I was desperate to get the TV going so I wouldn't miss the games, so I took it to the only repair shop open, thinking it might have been damaged in the move. They checked it out and said there was nothing wrong with it. So I took it back home, put it back in place, and tried again. I was getting really frustrated when my sister-in-law pointed to a switch on the wall and asked me, "What's this for?" Then she flipped the switch out of curiosity, and guess what happened. The TV came on! I asked her how she made that happen, and she said, "I flipped the switch!"

There was nothing wrong with the TV. I just needed to flip the switch to give it power.

Do You Feel Powerless?

Feeling powerless is one of the most frustrating and sometimes even terrifying experiences we have as humans. Whether we are being pushed around by a person in authority, seeing a loved one suffer through a health crisis we can't change, or feeling overwhelmed by the number of people suffering around the world, we hate feeling as if we have no control.

We might seek power to overcome limitations and insecurities or some other obstacle or challenge we face in life. For example, you may have dealt with infertility. You may need to overcome addiction, or maybe you have a wayward child. All of these make you feel powerless. But what does real power look like?

When I mention the word *power*, what comes to mind? Do you think of power as having a lot of money, being the CEO of a Fortune 500 company, leading a large organization? Is it being physically strong? Power can come in the form of physical strength, influence, money, knowledge, access, or some other way of controlling people, situations, and outcomes. But those are earthly definitions of *power*. God's power is going to help you overcome obstacles, difficulties, and challenges in life.

Power in God's Word

There are many examples in the Bible of people declaring the Word of God and His promises. This is because there is power in the speaking of God's Word over our lives. In fact, every time I stand up to preach, my prayer is that I will be faithful to communicate the truth of God's Word clearly and practically with boldness from the Holy Spirit. My words alone are limited, but when I speak the Word of God, the Holy Spirit changes people's lives. (See 1 Corinthians 2:4.) *There is power when we speak God's Word.*

When the Israelites were migrating to Canaan, they had been on a long journey and come up against a lot of obstacles and were pretty defeated and discouraged. During that time God called Joshua to lead His people the rest of the way into the Promised Land, but Joshua was afraid.

In Joshua 1:8–9 God tells Joshua to be strong and courageous and that having the Word of God in him would empower him for the challenges ahead:

> Study this Book of Instruction continually. Meditate on it day and night so you will be sure to obey everything written in it. Only then will you prosper and succeed in all you do. This is my command—be strong and courageous! Do not be afraid or discouraged. For the LORD your God is with you wherever you go.

The Bible is alive and powerful and sharper than any two-edged sword (Heb. 4:12). We need to get into God's Word and let His Word get into us.

Reading the Bible is the first step, but then we need to go beyond that and meditate on His Word. Psalm 1 says that when we meditate on God's Word, we will be fruitful like a tree planted by streams of water (vv. 2–3). We have to read it, meditate on it, and memorize it. Reading and memorizing Scripture is something most of us learn how to do at church, but not everyone understands how to incorporate the meditating part. Meditating on the Bible is more than just reading Scripture. It means reading it, thinking about how it applies to your life, praying it into your life, believing His promises, and keeping His Word in your heart.

How many times have you crammed for a test or presentation that required you to memorize information so you would be able to recite it later? I think nearly everyone has at some point. But can you say you actually retained that information after the exam? So much of the time we memorize things without actually thinking about what the information means and how it can be applied to other situations.

That's why meditation on Scripture is so important. It holds God's promises for us as well as His instruction. When we know what He has told us to do, we know better how to respond to negative situations we face in our lives. We also know all the blessings He has for us, and we are able to claim them. Anytime you face a difficult circumstance or have to make a choice in life, if you have meditated on Scripture, you will have God's Word accessible and will understand how to apply it in your life. Here are some examples of how the promises in Scripture can empower you to overcome any obstacle:

- When you are afraid, declare 2 Timothy 1:7: "For God has not given us a spirit of fear, but

of power and of love and of a sound mind"
(NKJV).

- When you feel trapped and as if there is no
  hope, declare Psalm 121:1–2: "Where does my
  help come from? My help comes from the
  LORD, the Maker of heaven and earth" (NIV).

- When you feel as if something is impossible,
  declare Philippians 4:13: "I can do all things
  through Christ who strengthens me" (NKJV).

- When you are discouraged, declare Psalm
  43:5: "Why am I discouraged? Why is my
  heart so sad? I will put my hope in God! I
  will praise him again—my Savior and my
  God!"

- When you feel all alone, declare Isaiah 43:2:
  "When you pass through the waters, I will
  be with you; and when you pass through
  the rivers, they will not sweep over you.
  When you walk through the fire, you will
  not be burned; the flames will not set you
  ablaze" (NIV).

- When you have a dream that seems beyond
  reality, declare Ephesians 3:20: "Now to
  him who is able to do immeasurably more

than all we ask or imagine, according to his power that is at work within us" (NIV).

- When you're in doubt, declare Ephesians 1:14: "The Spirit is God's guarantee that he will give us the inheritance he promised and that he has purchased us to be his own people. He did this so we would praise and glorify him."

God's Word holds so much power that speaking His promises over whatever you face can change everything for you. Read, meditate on, and memorize His Word, and begin speaking that power into your life.

GOD CAN BREATHE NEW LIFE INTO A DEAD SITUATION

Not only do God's words have power over our current and future situations, but also God can revitalize and restore things of the past that need healing.

In Ezekiel chapter 37 the Israelites had been conquered by the Babylonians. God's promise to make them a great nation seemed impossible based on what they had just experienced and their current circumstances. But God intended to fulfill His promise to restore them. He directed Ezekiel to prophesy the rebirth of Israel. Ezekiel 37:5 says, "This is what the Sovereign LORD says: Look! I am going to put breath into you and make you live again!" God's people had been defeated and were discouraged, and they were scattered throughout the region. But God was getting ready to do a new thing.

It can be easy to get stuck in the past, but God doesn't want us to stay there. He wants us to let go. He wants to redeem us. Forget what is behind you, and move on. He has the power to take what was and do something new.

In my years of ministry experience I've seen a lot of churches get stuck in the past, and I've found that we need to be more loyal to the future than the past. These churches may want to change and have a greater impact, but they don't realize they need to consider a new approach to reach their community. Trusting in the promise of God and the power of His desire to do something new is what led us to start C3. Although there weren't a lot of resources and we didn't know exactly what to do when we started the church, we trusted God to show us how to reach people where they live today.

We saw our world changing and believed we needed to meet God where He wanted to work. We saw so many people who were far from God, many of whom were not getting connected to the local church. So God called us to relocate and plant a church that would reach them where they live. Our desire was never to reach people who were already attending church, but to reach people who felt hopeless.

Our world has different issues than it did one hundred years ago, fifty years ago, or even ten years ago. Think about how much things have changed since September 11, 2001. This is why we believe it is important to communicate the unchanging Word of God in a way that hits where people are living today. In a time of such rapid change

God's unchanging Word provides the hope, healing, and restoration we need.

When Martha and I decided to come to Clayton to launch C3, we knew God was calling us to start a different kind of church that would create an environment of hope—one in which people who might think church isn't relevant and that Jesus can't help them could hear a different message. We believed God wanted us to create a place where He could breathe new life into others.

Just as God promised Ezekiel that He would breathe life into the Israelites so they could live again, He makes the same promise to us.

GOD WILL GIVE YOU SUPERNATURAL STRENGTH

When we are feeling defeated and discouraged the way the Israelites did, we also feel drained of emotional, mental, physical, and spiritual strength. At those times relying on our own power is not an option. That is when we must turn to God and begin speaking His promises.

When God was using the prophet Ezekiel to reassure the Israelites that He planned to restore them, as we read previously, He gave Ezekiel a vision:

> The LORD took hold of me, and I was carried away by the Spirit of the LORD to a valley filled with bones. He led me all around among the bones that covered the valley floor. They were scattered everywhere across the ground and were completely

dried out. Then he asked me, "Son of man, can these bones become living people again?"

"O Sovereign LORD," I replied, "you alone know the answer to that."

Then he said to me, "Speak a prophetic message to these bones and say, 'Dry bones, listen to the word of the LORD! This is what the Sovereign LORD says: Look! I am going to put breath into you and make you live again! I will put flesh and muscles on you and cover you with skin. I will put breath into you, and you will come to life. Then you will know that I am the LORD.'"

—EZEKIEL 37:1–6

God showed Ezekiel that His words had the power to restore life, and if Ezekiel spoke those words, God's power would flow through him. That was not everyday human power God was showing him. That was supernatural power—the kind that lets you know really clearly that it is God working through you.

What if everyone rose up and lived with boldness, cared with compassion, loved others who are different, and gave everything they had to Jesus? What kind of power would that generate for doing God's work to heal and restore what was dried up and dead in our lives? Incredible, unimaginable things can happen when we individually speak God's promises, so collectively raising our voices and speaking God's truth really could change the world for the better.

God pours this power into our lives on a daily basis.

But there is an even more important way that God's power impacts our lives, not just temporarily, but eternally.

The fifth "I am" declaration Jesus makes may be one of the most important for us. It certainly holds the most power: "*I am the resurrection and the life. Anyone who believes in me will live, even after dying*" (John 11:25, emphasis added). Jesus offers us renewal. He is greater than our enemy, the devil. In 1 John 4:4 the Bible tells us, "But you belong to God, my dear children. You have already won a victory over those people, because the Spirit who lives in you is greater than the spirit who lives in the world."

Jesus brings us back from the dark and powerless places we were in and into the light and life only He can offer.

He is the resurrection.

The Bible tells us that Jesus resurrected people. We don't know how many He actually raised from the dead, but three are recorded in the Gospels. The most notable of them is Lazarus—Jesus's best friend and the brother of Mary and Martha—who had been dead for four days by the time Jesus arrived.

Mary called for Jesus, but even though He was a short distance away, He waited two days to travel. Martha was upset with Jesus and didn't understand why He didn't come more quickly. To her it didn't make sense that Jesus would take so long to get there. By the time Jesus arrived, Lazarus was already dead:

Martha said to Jesus, "Lord, if only you had been here, my brother would not have died. But even now I know that God will give you whatever you ask."

Jesus told her, "Your brother will rise again."

"Yes," Martha said, "he will rise when everyone else rises, at the last day."

—John 11:21–24

It looked like Jesus was late, but He was right on time! Mary and Martha were grieving and upset that Jesus didn't come earlier. But Jesus had a plan. John 11:43–44 says:

Then Jesus shouted, "Lazarus, come out!" And the dead man came out, his hands and feet bound in graveclothes, his face wrapped in a headcloth. Jesus told them, "Unwrap him and let him go!"

Lazarus walked out of the grave and had new life! The Bible says that many became believers because of this event, and the Pharisees were furious and wanted to kill Jesus. This was Jesus's last recorded miracle and took place only one month before His own resurrection.

Jesus went on to explain to Martha:

"I am the resurrection and the life. Anyone who believes in me will live, even after dying. Everyone who lives in me and believes in me will never ever die. Do you believe this, Martha?"

"Yes, Lord," she told him. "I have always

believed you are the Messiah, the Son of God, the
one who has come into the world from God."

—JOHN 11:25–27

But Jesus wasn't referring to some future experience. He
was declaring that He *is* the resurrection and the life right
now. It's who He is and the fulfillment of
why He came.

Not only would Jesus rise from the grave,
but He is the resurrection. What Jesus was
trying to help Martha grasp was that her understanding of what would happen to believers
in Jesus after they died was happening in the
here and now. Jesus was moving resurrection from a belief
system—an idea to put faith in—to a person—a Savior to
put your trust in. He was trying to shift her thinking from
the future to the present.

The same power that raised Christ from the grave is available to you and me.

Jesus was trying to explain that belief in Him isn't
another religion with a statement of faith. Christianity isn't
merely a *religion* with dos and don'ts; it's a *relationship*
with the risen Christ. Christianity *is* Christ!

Resurrection leads to life. So if you are a believer, you
can't help but be filled with life and passion. Our God is
not dead. He's alive! And the devil doesn't have a chance
against us when we are filled with His resurrection power.

You need to know that God's resurrection power is available to us today. The same power that raised Christ from
the grave is available to you and me. I don't doubt for one
second that if God thought it was necessary to actually

bring someone back to life, He could do it. But it's more important for us to understand what *resurrection* means on a spiritual level than on a physical one.

Our spiritual deaths are way more devastating than our physical ones. That's because when we don't know God, the death of our earthly bodies means our souls are permanently separated from Him.

The reality is that there are only two options after we die—heaven or hell. The unfortunate reality is that if we don't choose Jesus, we spend eternity separate from Him forever.

Faith is believing without seeing. And the kind of resurrection we need is to be brought back from the death that results from not having faith in Jesus. We need to be resurrected into new life in Christ.

He is the Life.

I have a dog name Zoe. One day when she was just a puppy, she got into our vitamins. She had chewed them up and had the residue all over her face. We were a little worried that they might hurt her, but then we realized we take vitamins to make us healthier, so they couldn't be too bad. When I took her outside, she ran in circles all over the backyard.

Vitamins are important for our physical well-being. Martha makes me take a handful of them every day because they improve my health, boost my energy, and will help keep me around for a long, full life. But we also need to do things such as attend church, read the Bible, pray, and worship to strengthen our spiritual health to enrich our lives and what comes after.

The Greek word for life is *zōē*. It's used thirty-six times in the Gospel of John alone. The word basically means "possessed of vitality," which is where we get the word for *vitamin*.[1]

God sent His Holy Spirit to fill us with power, which is far more than any vitamin could ever do. He has come to give you eternal life and abundant life. Jesus is the only One who can give you real life.

Maybe you've tried to find real life by filling the void with money, possessions, and relationships. Or maybe you have regrets of past mistakes and are wondering if you ever could have the life that God wants you to experience.

He is the God who will give you a fresh start! I'm so thankful that He is the God of second chances and is always waiting to give you a fresh start. There is no life so far gone that God can't breathe life into it. As 2 Corinthians 5:17 says, "Therefore, if anyone is in Christ, the new creation has come: The old has gone, the new is here!" (NIV).

Paul's Story
Jesus Is Your Strength When You Feel Helpless

My wife, Pat, and I moved from a small mill town in Maine called Millinocket, where I was born and lived for forty-nine years. I worked at a paper mill and raised my family there until a workplace injury crippled me. I found the long winters were too much for me to bear, and Pat had an opportunity to relocate with her job to North Carolina, so we left Maine. We had no idea where to go, but for some reason we chose Raleigh. We were in a new place and didn't know anybody.

When Pat started her new job, I just stayed home, enjoying the sunshine. My wife was on me all the time to find a church to attend, as my doctors told us there was nothing they could do for me and that by the age of sixty I would be confined to a wheelchair, so I should try to find a church where I could volunteer just to keep my mind off my injuries and pain. But I really felt things were fine and that I could handle the pain on my own without church or anyone else, so I kept fighting her about finding a church.

I made every excuse I could think of to get her off my back about church—it was too hot, it was too cold, I did not feel good, my back hurt, and so on. Then one day we were driving past this little school called Cleveland Elementary School, and I saw the church sign. I said to Pat, "Hey, we could go there," thinking she wouldn't want to go there and that the suggestion would get her off my back about church. Well, I was wrong, and she said it would be OK to visit, so I had to attend church that Sunday.

Looking back, I realize the reason I didn't want to go to church was fear. I really believed that everyone there knew all about God and the Bible when I knew nothing, and I did not want to look stupid about Christianity even though I was. Nothing in the Bible made any sense to me, and I really felt out of place and uncomfortable in church. When we visited, I quickly noticed a lot of teenagers who were really enjoying the music. They were singing and clapping and seemed to be having a good time, and it dawned on me that maybe there was hope for us all if these teens were not moaning because their parents made them be there. They were really happy to be there. I think that was what made me want to visit again. Plus, everybody there was as nice as could be, and it made me want to go back.

Shortly after that Pat and I started serving in the church. I helped out with the children's ministry, and Pat helped serve coffee and donuts in the café and helped out at the small library. We attended the first connect group led by Pastor Matt Fry and his wife, Martha. It was there that I wrote down the story of my salvation—how and when I accepted Jesus Christ into my life— and I gave it to Pastor Matt. A short time later Pastor Matt asked me if I wanted to be baptized, and I said yes. The following Sunday after church we went to a subdivision with a swimming pool, and I was the first person Pastor Matt baptized at C3 Church.

It wasn't long after that a group of men went to Raleigh for a men's retreat. This was a powerful weekend with a strong group of Christian men. I had never been involved in anything like that, but I really enjoyed it. The second day of the retreat we started praying at 5:45 a.m., and after praying for two hours, one of the leaders told us that God had laid it on his heart to pray for someone to be healed. He set up pastors at various stations to pray for everyone, starting with our minds and moving on to our eyes, our ears, our mouths, our hearts, our hands, and our feet. Because I had to use a cane and was very slow, I was the last person to receive prayer. All the pastors who had been praying at the various stations came over and laid hands on my feet, and I don't even know why, but I just held my hands out and told God, "Whatever You will."

The retreat was quite different from anything I had ever been involved in before. When I got home, I told my wife about the prayer time, and she said that sounded interesting. The next morning I was in the backyard having coffee when my wife stepped outside and gave me a very strange look. I asked her what was wrong, and she said, "Look at you. I haven't seen you move like that for twelve years." And it wasn't until then that I realized I didn't have my cane. For twelve years I needed my cane just to get up from bed and get dressed. Not only had Jesus laid His hands on me in the night and healed my pain, but also He had erased the fact that I needed my cane.

Sometime later Pastor Matt asked me if I would be interested in maintaining and overseeing the new facilities we were about to move into, and I prayed about it. I knew God had healed me for a reason, and this was it. I not only oversaw facilities but also taught the four-year-olds about Jesus for several years.

I once was crippled, but now I'm healed. I was lost but now am found. I have a Savior named Jesus, who loves me and watches over me, and there isn't anything I can't do through Him and with Him. I couldn't do it myself as I thought, but God doesn't want us to do life alone. We really do need one another to make it in this world.

We all have times in our lives when we feel powerless. It might be because we feel lost and alone. It could be that we have suffered an illness or injury that has robbed us of our strength. We might just feel emotionally weak from difficulties in life. But as Paul pointed out in 1 Corinthians 12, God doesn't want us to go through life alone. He wants us to lean on one another and build a network of support to lift one another up. But even more important, He wants us to lean on Him. He is the resurrection and the Life that renews us every day and empowers us to fulfill our purpose.

NEXT STEPS

Read Acts 1:6–8:

> So when they had come together, they asked Him, "Lord, will You at this time restore the kingdom to Israel?" He said to them, "It is not for you to know the times or the dates, which the Father has fixed by His own authority. But you shall receive power when the Holy Spirit comes upon you. And you shall be My witnesses in Jerusalem, and in all Judea and Samaria, and to the ends of the earth."
>
> —MEV

Reflect:

- According to this passage, what do we receive power to do?

- Do you remember a time in your life when you felt powerless? Were there ways you tried to compensate for that feeling of powerlessness?

- How is that experience of feeling powerless impacting your life today?

Declare:

God, Your power is available to me through Your Holy Spirit. I receive Your power so I can live the life You have planned for me. You are for me. You have great plans and a purpose for my life.

Chapter Six

Do You Need More of God?

I Am the Way, the Truth, and the Life

I am the way, the truth, and the life. No one
can come to the Father except through me.
—John 14:6

ONE OF THE great things about attending college is
that it allows you to step outside the small bubble you
existed in as a kid. You are exposed to people who think
differently, have different life experiences, and like different things. A lot of that is really good for your personal
growth, but sometimes it can be tough to navigate all of
those new options as a young person and know what is
true and worth having in your life.

I've worked with lots of people who have struggled to
determine what direction they should take in life or which

decision to make. Do I go to college, or try to find a job right away? Do I get married, or take some time to see what else is out there? Do I risk moving across the country for this career opportunity?

You may not be able to relate to being called to serve God as a pastor or missionary, or in some other role in a church or religious organization. In fact, you may not even know anyone who has felt led in that direction. But the choice to commit your life to someone or something is a big one no matter what the circumstance, and trying to do so without the help of good counsel makes the decision that much more intimidating. Anxiety over making the wrong choice might tempt you to avoid making a decision for as long as you can. Many people would rather not deal with a situation than have to make a hard choice. But we can't avoid the major decisions of life forever.

I knew when I was a teenager that God was calling me to serve Him. I didn't know exactly what I was feeling, but I can recall going to the altar in the Baptist church we attended and saying, "I will go and do whatever for You." I remember sensing that God had big plans for me. As time went by, even though the seeds of His calling for my life were planted in my heart, I was afraid that if I totally surrendered my life to God, I would have to go into the ministry and my life would be miserable. So in many ways I ran from God during my high school years. In college I was still running from Him with no plans of going into the ministry. But God was pursuing me all along. During my freshman year of college, when I realized that God is who He says He is and that Jesus rose from the grave, I completely surrendered my life to Christ, and I've never been the same since.

I went to college thinking I was running from God, and I actually ran right to Him. I immediately started serving in ministry and began to realize that when I lean into God, He leans back into me. And leaning into God—seeking more of Him—is how you can find your way through difficult circumstances, periods of doubt, and big decisions. Understanding this fact made a huge difference in my life. Realizing that He will be there to guide and support us is the greatest knowledge we can have as we make our way through life.

The reality is, when you find God, you have it all. You don't need to keep searching.

ARE YOU STRUGGLING TO FIND YOUR WAY?

Maybe you feel as if you've been fumbling through life, struggling to find your way, having a hard time knowing what is true. I think we all face this at some point in our lives. We may get lots of opinions and advice on what to do, but there is only one way to really get where we need to be. We need to know the Way, meaning we need to experience more of God. And to experience more of God, we have to know God personally.

You should know that getting "more of God" is a tough proposition because it definitely means changing the way we are living our lives. A lot of us are comfortable where we are, or at least anxious about moving into something unknown. However, experiencing more of God is the way to get out of a comfort zone you may have settled into that isn't good for you.

Whether you know God and have long been involved in church, are just beginning your relationship with Him, or have never prayed before in your life, it is essential for you to draw closer to God and understand the ways He can work in your life. And the more of God you invite into your life, the more blessings you will experience.

More hope

It is easy to get bogged down in worrying about taking care of bills and children and jobs. Earlier in this book I shared with you the story of when I was unexpectedly unemployed. I lost my job and didn't know what my future held. I felt hopeless and didn't know where to turn. I questioned God and wondered how He could have let this happen when I was doing my best to serve Him. I couldn't see past the fear over how I would support my family. But God had greater things in store for me.

> "For I know the plans I have for you," says the Lord. "They are plans for good and not for disaster, to give you a future and a hope."
> —Jeremiah 29:11

Maybe you can relate to this. Here is a promise from God that has helped me through times like that one: "'For I know the plans I have for you,' says the Lord. 'They are plans for good and not for disaster, to give you a future and a hope'" (Jer. 29:11).

No matter how dark and hopeless things look, we can

be assured that even if we face failure, God can use it to strengthen and teach us. But we have to draw closer to Him. We must seek Him more to know how to move toward what He intends for us to have next and to receive the hope that will sustain us until His plans unfold in His time.

More comfort

Do you have a favorite comfort food? My grandma was from England, so my mom passed on to me a love for hot tea. Whenever I was sick and needed comforting, a cup of hot tea with cream and sugar along with a piece of toast with peanut butter and jelly would do the trick. To this day if I'm not feeling well, I can just fix a cup of English Breakfast Tea and a piece of toast, and it somehow makes everything a little better. There's nothing wrong with finding these kinds of things soothing, but real comfort—the kind that really settles your soul—doesn't come from temporary fixes like this.

We look for different ways to comfort ourselves when we are worried, upset, or scared, and we can also end up turning to things that actually harm us in the long run. When our church was losing the space where we met and we didn't know what to do, some were tempted to try to force the school to let us stay. We might have felt proactive if we had done that, but we would not have ended up with a good situation. Instead, we turned to God for answers. Of course He led us to a solution, but by leaning on Him for guidance and support, we also received His comfort as we waited for the answer to come together in His perfect timing.

The Bible says, "Come to Me, all you who labor and are heavily burdened, and I will give you rest" (Matt. 11:28, MEV). The rest this verse is referring to doesn't mean to just take a nap. Jesus is saying He will give us comfort when we are weighed down with burdens. If we give our concerns over to Him and trust Him to take care of them, we can sleep peacefully, work productively, and relax and enjoy our families and friends the way God wants us to.

More wisdom

How many times have you cried out to anyone who may be listening, "I don't know what to do; somebody tell me which way to go"? I think we all have at some point. We all face decisions that have either no clear options or no good ones. Knowing how to proceed in these situations can feel really overwhelming. You might even end up paralyzed, afraid of making a move in any direction.

> Come to Me, all you who labor and are heavily burdened, and I will give you rest.
> —Matthew 11:28, MEV

As a pastor I have a lot of people come to me for guidance and counsel in handling all kinds of relationship troubles—marriage, parenting, friendships, career—and ask how they should or shouldn't act in various situations. They are looking for wisdom, and I'll be honest, if I had to rely on myself, I probably wouldn't get very far with them. The same is true in my own life. I don't have all the answers, but I do know where to go to get them. Whether it is for me or for someone who comes to me, I know I have to search God's Word and spend time in prayer to receive the kind of wisdom that will do more than just fix a situation, but will heal, restore, enhance, and bless it.

James 1:5 says that if we lack wisdom, we should ask God, and He will give it to us generously. Before you ask someone else his opinion, go to God and ask Him! That means take everything to God, and seek His wisdom. And it means to pray and study the guidance the Bible gives for how to deal with every aspect of life.

More strength

Whether you need to endure a trial, stand up for yourself or someone else, make change happen, or overcome an obstacle, you need strength. None of us has the ability to do any of these things on our own and experience lasting, life-changing results.

A lot of people take pride in their ability to be independent and self-sufficient. They have great confidence in their own strength. Maybe they spend every day at the gym building their muscles so they won't have to feel weak physically. They could be the type to put in eighty hours a week at their jobs and who save and invest to build up a big bank account so they don't feel weak financially. Or maybe they shut people out, do everything for themselves, and put up walls to protect against vulnerability so they don't feel weak emotionally.

No matter what kind of weakness we are trying to avoid or overcome, none of that is going to be resolved by our own efforts. Everything we accomplish in life is done through the power God pours into us. When we have more of God, we don't ever have to fear being beaten in a physical match because we know God is our greatest protector. We don't have to worry about financial security because we know our needs will be met. And we don't have to run from relationships because God can help heal our wounds.

The Bible says, "I can do all things through Christ who strengthens me" (Phil. 4:13, NKJV). Letting God be your strength gives you so much more than just a temporary way to overcome the challenges you face in life. It strengthens you so you are equipped for anything you will encounter.

More patience

How many times have you heard someone say, "God, give me patience"? We ask for patience to deal with difficult people, to wait for things we know are coming, and to wait for answers when we don't know what's ahead.

> **I can do all things through Christ who strengthens me.
> –Philippians 4:13, NKJV**

Being patient is one of the hardest things for us to do as humans. Even in the best of circumstances we still get impatient if it feels as if things are taking too long. But when we feel desperate, it can be nearly impossible to sit and wait because we feel alone and in the dark. When I lost my job and had no idea what was coming next, I struggled with wanting to try to force God's hand. I needed answers, and I needed them yesterday. I couldn't just sit back and wait for God to show me how to move forward, but that's exactly what I needed to do. God had a plan for my life, and He was working in my life to bring great things that I couldn't see coming. That's why I should have been patient with Him. All I had was the tunnel-vision view of disappointment ahead of me. He had the bird's-eye, 360-degree view. He saw not just my life but how my life connected to other people's lives as well.

When we are able to be patient and let God do His thing, we open ourselves up to so much more than we could have anticipated. And the more we do that, the more patience we develop for future situations. Galatians 5:22 says, "But the fruit of the Spirit is love, joy, peace, patience, gentleness, goodness, faith" (MEV). All of those things come from being in the Spirit—being closer to God—and seeking more of Him.

More peace

Wanting to have peace is a universal desire. *Peace* here refers to personal, inner peace that keeps you from worrying or being anxious. It also means being at peace with the people around you so there isn't negativity and arguing. And it includes the really big desire for world peace that people talk about so we can stop the wars and suffering.

There is a powerful picture that illustrates what having true peace means—the kind of peace that can be found only by having more of God. In the picture there is a bird sitting on a branch as storms rage all around it. The message is that peace isn't a calm, tranquil lake where nothing bad is happening. Peace is being able to be calm and still even when there is turmoil all around you.

Anyone can feel peaceful when nothing is going wrong; it takes God's hand on your life and His presence in your heart to have peace even when you are struggling and facing difficult times. "You will keep in perfect peace all who trust in you, all whose thoughts are fixed on you!" (Isa. 26:3). When we draw closer to God and keep our thoughts fixed on Him, we get to experience more of the peace He provides, which will help us weather any storm.

More joy

God's Word says the joy of the Lord is our strength (Neh. 8:10). When we are filled with God's joy, He gives us the strength that we need. A lot of people equate joy with happiness, but the two aren't the same. Happiness is an emotion you feel when something positive happens— when someone makes you laugh, when you've had a good day, or when you are doing something you love. Happiness almost always happens because something external triggered that feeling. It sends you on a roller coaster of emotions. Happiness is about happenings, but joy is different. Joy is internal and lasting. The joy that comes from the Holy Spirit is continuous. And being joyful can happen even in difficult situations. No matter what is happening around you, God's joy that comes from the inside gives you strength to live out His purpose for your life.

There were many times when I was enjoying what God was doing in my life. Then, as soon as I faced an obstacle, I would begin to question God and wonder why He hadn't intervened and where He had gone. It wasn't until

I realized that God was with me through all of it and I had just been taking my eyes off of Him that I was able to experience joy in the midst of tough situations. I haven't stopped facing challenges; I just know now that God has everything under control. Not only can I be joyful when I am in the middle of a crisis or experiencing growing pains, but I can actually be joyful for them because I know God is working out great things through whatever is happening.

Inviting God to fill my life and having more of Him in every area have allowed me to know the truth of this verse: "You will show me the way of life, granting me the joy of your presence and the pleasures of living with you forever" (Ps. 16:11). As I have sought more of God, He has shown and continues to show me how He is the Way, the Truth, and the Life I need to experience the most abundant life.

JESUS IS THE WAY

I used to think that religion was about trying really hard and being really good. I thought if I did good things, God would love me, and if I was bad, He would be mad at me. I tried to live for God and would do OK with it for a little while and then fall away. During my freshman year in college I began questioning my faith. Why do I believe what I believe? Is it just because of the way I was raised, or is what I've been taught really true? God gave me the answers I needed.

> **You will show me the way of life, granting me the joy of your presence and the pleasures of living with you forever.**
> **—Psalm 16:11**

I'll never forget it. I was sitting in Dr. Gary Habermas's

Philosophy 101 class, and he began to explain why the Resurrection is a historical fact. I discovered then that we base our faith on the truth of the death, burial, and resurrection of Jesus. After that I dove into God's Word and got counsel from some older Christians. It was during this time that I realized for myself that Jesus really is who He says He is.

I went from an inherited faith to a personal faith. Now Jesus was real to me! The Bible really was the truth, and He truly was *the Way*. The gospel was something that actually would bring me eternal life, and I could put my whole faith in it. That realization caused me to fall in love with Jesus and discover that I could stop trying and start trusting in the One who lived, died, and rose from the grave for me!

This was an important moment for me. I went from believing in Jesus because that's how I was raised to knowing Jesus is real and having an intimate, personal relationship with God. I remember crying out to God during that time, saying, "Lord, I need more of You!" I told Him I wanted to surrender my life to Him and to live out His plan and purpose for my life. I was so tired of running and trying to avoid what I was feeling Him calling me to do, and it was a huge relief to give myself over to God and open myself up to receiving more of Him.

When I read this verse from John, I finally understood what was required of me: "He must become greater and greater, and I must become less and less. He has come from above and is greater than anyone else" (John 3:30–31). I had to set aside my expectations, demands, and disappointments and lean into Him in order to discover the life I was supposed to have.

It all comes down to what Jesus said in John 14:6: "*I am the way, the truth, and the life.* No one can come to the Father except through me" (emphasis added).

Coming to the huge realization that Jesus really is who the Bible says He is was not as easy as it might seem considering the fact that I grew up in church. I'm not sure what exactly held me back, but I think it had something to do with the fact that I knew if I really bought into everything I had been taught, my life was going to change in ways I was afraid I wasn't ready for. If Jesus really is all He said He is, I would have to give myself over to Him completely, and I wasn't sure what that kind of commitment meant. I'm glad I chose to take the risk and go all in. It has been more than worth it.

When Martha and I were expecting our first of three children, we were nervous, as any new parents are. We received lots of advice from lots of people. Some of it we asked for, but a lot of it was unsolicited. We ended up discovering a book about parenting that gave us the kind of guidance we thought would be right for us. We followed the suggestions for one of the most important parts of parenting—getting your child to sleep through the night. And it worked! Really well. But there were people who didn't think the book was telling us the right way to do things. We could have easily gotten into debates about what the best method was, but that wouldn't have been productive.

Our way worked for us, and everyone involved decided to agree to disagree.

The thing is when it comes to parenting, there can be more than one way to do things. But when it comes to getting to heaven, there is only one Way. That Way is Jesus. You can debate that issue as much as you want, but only one thing is true: Jesus is not just *a* way; Jesus is *the* Way—the Way to our heavenly Father, the Way to eternal life.

Think about this: If you go to the grave of Buddha, his bones are still there. If you go to the grave of Muhammad, his bones are still there. But if you go to the grave of Jesus— if you look in His tomb—He is not there. He has risen, just as He said He would!

All roads don't lead to heaven. There are some who believe you can pick any god and end up in heaven. That may be politically correct, but it's not biblically correct! That may sound like a good idea, but there's one problem: it's not the truth!

Jesus Is the Truth

All of Christianity is built around three critical truths: the miracle of the Cross, the miracle of Jesus's death, and the miracle of His Resurrection! It's the miracle of the Resurrection that separates Christianity from all other religions. Jesus is the only One who claimed to be God and said He would die on the cross and be raised from the grave three days later. And as it was prophesied hundreds of years before, He did just that!

Jesus is the Way, but He is more than that. He's also the

Truth! We don't base our faith on a myth. Our faith is not blind; it is based on Truth. There was a man named Jesus Christ who walked this earth, claimed to be the Messiah, performed miracles, died on the cross, rose from the grave on the third day, and has returned to heaven to prepare a place for us! There are a number of books out there by Bible scholars who present all the evidence really well, so I'm not going to spend a lot of time making the case for Jesus. But I will share a few points with you:

- Historical support: There are more than three hundred history accounts written during the time of the Bible that verify Jesus rose from the grave.[1]

- Documented eyewitness accounts: There were eyewitnesses who saw and wrote about Jesus, such as His disciples. Jesus lived and worked with them; He didn't just make pop-in appearances. (See John 21.)

- Scriptural evidence: The Bible records many different settings where Jesus was seen after the Resurrection. Jesus was on earth for forty days after His death and continued to appear to people and tell them about the kingdom of God. (See Acts 1:3.)

So not only was there a man named Jesus who lived and walked the earth, healing the sick, ministering to those in need, and raising people from the dead—He also was resurrected and walked around the streets of Jerusalem for forty days. How would you like to be those religious leaders who put Jesus to death? "You know that guy you just crucified? He's back!"

I can only imagine how John felt when he wrote these words from Revelation 1:17–18:

> When I saw him, I fell at his feet as if I were dead. But he laid his right hand on me and said, "Don't be afraid! I am the First and the Last. I am the living one. I died, but look—I am alive forever and ever! And I hold the keys of death and the grave."

Jesus is the First and the Last—the living One. He died but is now alive forever and ever! I think I understood that on some level when I was young. But I didn't get what a big deal it was until I begged God for more of Him.

Josh McDowell famously made the argument that Jesus had to be the true Lord, a lunatic, or a liar, and most of the people you encounter are going to fall into one of those camps in their opinions about Jesus. Some will say He was delusional and lived in a fantasy world; others think He was making up everything He claimed. You may also find people who think He was a good person who had good teachings, but who don't think He was really the Son of God, as He said.

But they're wrong. There is proof He existed. There is

evidence that people believed He is who He said He is and that He backed it up in the ways He touched their lives. What you believe about Him is up to you. It is up to you to decide if you will let Him be Lord of your life. But there is no greater life than the one you will experience by accepting Him.

Jesus Is the Life

In the Garden of Eden, Adam and Eve had it made. They were in paradise. And they were both beautiful and had no problems—no debt, no stress, no bills, no exes, no children, no in-laws, and no clothes!

The only thing God told them they couldn't do was eat the fruit from one tree. He gave them everything they could possibly need or want and only one restriction. You'd think that would be an easy way to get by in life, right? Well, they managed to mess it up.

The devil lied to them. Eve took the bait of Satan and ate some of the forbidden fruit. Then she gave it to Adam, and he ate it. All of a sudden they realized they were naked and had sinned. Adam blamed Eve, Eve blamed the devil, and we've been playing the blame game ever since.

They had a beautiful and perfect life. I mean, it really was about as perfect as it gets because it was before sin corrupted the earth and before our human nature really started getting in the way—before we were fallen. All they had to do was embrace the life they were given and resist temptation. All they had to do was choose God's way, and they could have had a truly abundant life. Do you realize we are presented with the same choice? When we choose Jesus, we choose life!

When I was running from God in college and trying hard to avoid what He was calling me to do, I thought I was escaping something that was going to make my life really difficult and complicated. I thought I was getting away from something I didn't want. I didn't realize that I was running from the abundant life God wanted to give me.

By refusing to listen to God's call to me, I was failing to hear what He was trying to tell me: "I came that you may have life, and have it abundantly!" I was missing out on all the blessings and the richness of life God wanted to give me because I wanted to live my life my way, according to my truth. And that only marginally involved God.

When I finally realized what it meant for Jesus to truly be the Way, I knew my life would be empty without Him. That's when I cried out for more of God, and He began pouring into my life in amazing ways.

The thief comes only to steal and kill and destroy; I came that they may have life, and have it abundantly. –John 10:10, NASB

Understanding exactly what it means for Jesus to be the Way, the Truth, and the Life will cause you to want more of God, but it works in reverse too. Asking God for more of Himself will cause you to know more fully that He is the Way, the Truth, and the Life. This is the kind of fresh encounter with God that I mentioned in the introduction, and it's the kind of encounter that truly helps you begin to understand who you are.

Anisa's Story
Press Into God; Don't Pull Away

When Alan and I first met, Alan was going through a divorce and was an active drug user. He was still working but was addicted to crack cocaine. I was married, but I used the term loosely. I was not committed to my marriage and was attracted to Alan. I separated from my husband and began a nasty separation/divorce—my second divorce—as a single mom with two boys. During this time I was seeing Alan and was on track to have another unhealthy relationship. I was working two or three jobs. My relationship with my ex-husband was volatile, and I ended up getting arrested for assault and battery after having an altercation with him while trying to pick up my boys. I was not a good mom during this time and was focused only on me and my relationships.

Alan and I moved in together after we had been dating a few months, and he quit using drugs. We were married in 1997 and were having a great time, going to the beach almost every weekend and being on the lake on the weekends we weren't at the beach. We were basically just living for the weekends.

In 2001 we moved close to C3 Church. We saw signs for the church while we were out riding our bikes. Around this time someone was talking about going to church, and our daughter, Shelby, who was three at the time, asked why we didn't have a church. We couldn't answer her. Alan and I both had been raised in church, but we both quit attending as teenagers.

So that next Sunday I, along with my two boys and Shelby, went to C3 Church, which was meeting in a local elementary school. As soon as I walked in, I was overcome with emotion as volunteers helped me find the classes for my kids and then the cafeteria/worship center. I cried all through the worship service. I went home and told Alan he could dress casually and come to this church. He came the next weekend and found out he could wear shorts and flip-flops, and we haven't looked back.

The very week Alan came with us to church, one of the ministers on staff came over to talk with us, and Alan and I both rededicated our lives to the Lord. We prayed for our lives and our home to make a difference, though we had no idea what that would look like. We immediately began serving even though we had no idea what to do or how to serve. We just started by handing out worship programs in the lobby. Since then we have served in almost every area—from parking cars, ushering, helping to make coffee, and working in preschool and elementary classes to leading connect groups.

By attending various connect groups such as the freedom groups, we have dealt with issues in our past and are still learning to understand why we react the way we do, and we are discovering how to overcome strongholds. We also have learned that God does use all things for good. Alan leads a recovery group here at C3. We know firsthand that God does redeem the years the locusts have eaten because now Alan is helping others walk a road to recovery, which includes God as the source of their strength to overcome addiction.

I now get to help ladies overcome strongholds by helping with freedom groups. I also get to serve on staff! Me—twice divorced and arrested for assault and battery. Yes, God does use ordinary people.

That prayer of asking God to use us and our home has also become a reality. We have been a host home for countless connect groups, student weekend events, and more. We help people who need a place to start over by bringing them into our home to stay with us for a while. We believe God gave us second, third, fourth, and many more chances, and we now live on mission and on purpose to do the same for others.

And those years I didn't do the parenting thing so well? God has restored those years by giving me the opportunity to apologize to my boys and ask them for forgiveness. God now allows us to be spiritual parents and stand in the gap for those who live with us. We believe in seeing people the way God saw us—through His eyes of love. Through all our bad choices He saw our potential. Just as God never gave up on us, we want to show people that we care about them, love them unconditionally, and will never give up on them.

I'm happy to say Alan and I celebrate our twentieth wedding anniversary in 2017, and we have been faithful to each other through those twenty years! We have four kids (all of whom were saved and baptized at C3 Church) and two grandkids. Has life been easy since coming to C3? No, not always. Do we still have struggles? Yes, but there is peace through them all. We are so thankful that God led us to C3, where we were loved and accepted and where God met us and saved us for a holy life.

I mentioned that I work on staff at C3, but I have to explain that this is the second time. I worked on staff at C3 for a few years previously but left in an unhealthy state. I had allowed my heart to harden even while serving on staff. I wasn't spending time in God's Word. I was just worrying about the tasks at hand. When I left the staff, I left angry. Alan, however, remained firm that God had not released us from C3 Church. We stayed

planted and attended church even on the days I
didn't want to be there. Over time when I allowed
my heart to soften and let God start doing a work
in me, I began to want to be at church. I engaged
in worship, and I wanted to serve.

By our pressing in through the hard times
and remaining planted, God has given us some
great opportunities. Not only did I get the
chance to work on staff again, but I have had
opportunities to go on several mission trips to
Africa and Haiti. Alan and I even went on the last
mission trip to South Africa together. By simply
staying planted, we have seen God bless us and
our family beyond our wildest expectations.

Anisa discovered through her ups and downs that she
really does need more of God in her life. She learned that
Jesus is the Way, the Truth, and the Life, but that wasn't
enough to keep her from stumbling when she faced challenges. She realized that she had to draw closer to God. She
needed more than what she would get just by attending worship services and doing the work of the church. We all need
to find the way that Jesus provides, to know the truth that
He is Lord, and to live the life that comes from seeking
more of God.

NEXT STEPS

Read 2 Corinthians 1:3–5:

Praise be to the God and Father of our Lord Jesus Christ, the Father of compassion and the God of all comfort, who comforts us in all our troubles, so that we can comfort those in any trouble with the comfort we ourselves receive from God. For just as we share abundantly in the sufferings of Christ, so also our comfort abounds through Christ.

—NIV

Reflect:

- What is the cycle of comfort that is being described in this verse?

- What is something God has helped you overcome?

- Do you know somebody who is struggling, someone you could reach out to and help in his or her time of trouble?

Declare:

God, You never leave me nor forsake me. You comfort me in all my trouble. What the enemy meant for evil in my life You turn around for good.

Chapter Seven

Are You Connected?

I Am the Vine

> Yes, I am the vine; you are the
> branches. Those who remain in me, and
> I in them, will produce much fruit. For
> apart from me you can do nothing.
> —John 15:5

AFTER I FINISHED college and started working on my graduate degree, I was offered a youth pastor position in a large Southern city. I was so excited to live in a big city after having lived in a small college town. I jumped in with both feet serving the church. It was an exciting time as God began to move in our student ministry. We saw youths creating high school campus clubs, students being impacted, and incredible growth taking place.

At the time there weren't any women in the church whom I wanted to date, and I wasn't sure if it would be healthy for me to date someone within the congregation anyway. I went to other church singles events and felt so lonely. I would meet different girls, and we'd go out once, maybe twice, and that would be all. I knew God had big plans for me, and I wanted a wife who was headed in the same direction. At times I was so discouraged that I was still single. Most of my friends were married already, some were even having kids, and I couldn't even get a date for Friday night!

I remember crying out to God and asking, "Why am I still single?" I was feeling so lonely and hopeless that I became preoccupied with the girls I had dated. I would ask, "God, is she the one?" Then one day I felt God speak to me and say, "Matt, chill out! Stop being so anxious about who you are going to marry." (At least that's my interpretation of what He said.)

I prayed, "Lord, I am willing to be single the rest of my life if that's Your will. (P.S. God, I hope it's not.) But I would rather be single the rest of my life than get ahead of You and marry the wrong person." It was a moment I'll never forget. A peace came over me, and I became content in my relationship with God. I no longer needed a relationship to fill the void. God was more than enough.

A short time later an old friend moved to my city, and we began hanging out as friends. A few months later we started dating, and a few months after that we got engaged. We've now been faithfully married for twenty-four years and have three awesome children who love God. I had the privilege of baptizing all three of my kids. Looking back now, I am so glad I didn't get ahead of God and marry the wrong person.

In time friendship turned into a dating relationship, and now we are happily married and have three amazing children together. Our relationship is strong because it is God-centered. But I know I would not have been able to start, much less build, the kind of relationship we have if I hadn't been connected to God first.

Do You Feel Disconnected?

Have you moved to a new city for work or school where you feel lonely and disconnected? Are you struggling with being single as I did? You might even be married or surrounded by lots of friends and family and still feel alone. Do you know why? It's because you aren't connected to God in a way that will restore you and fulfill you.

Only God can fill the void in our lives in a lasting way. No matter how hard they might try or how good their intentions might be, people make mistakes, and they are going to let us down. That's just part of being human. It's only our connection to God that feeds us with the kind of strength and love that will sustain us through any circumstances we face in life.

Becoming Connected to God

Perhaps you are new to a relationship with God, or maybe you have spent years going to church and have never really felt you are getting from it what others are. Or you could be in a place where you don't know anything about God, and all of this sounds really strange to you. If you don't already have a connection with God, you may wonder how that even works.

In the previous chapter we talked about needing more of God and how I really struggled to understand what it means for God to be the Way, the Truth, and the Life. It had all been explained to me when I was growing up in church, but it wasn't something I really felt in my heart until I reached a pivotal moment that caused me to surrender to Him and cry out for Him. What happened in that moment was I became connected to God. I went from having head knowledge about Him to having heart knowledge—I felt Him in my life and in my heart. Instead of just accepting that God existed because people told me He did, I came to know He was real because I experienced connection with Him.

I went from having head knowledge about Him to having heart knowledge.

The reason Jesus used a vine as an analogy for the family of believers is that it was something to which people could easily relate. Other than water, wine was what people primarily drank during that time in that part of the world. Jesus used something very familiar not just to help His followers understand the fact that they were connected but also to really illustrate the kind of relationship He wanted with them. He said:

> I am the true grapevine, and my Father is the gardener. He cuts off every branch of mine that

doesn't produce fruit, and he prunes the branches that do bear fruit so they will produce even more. You have already been pruned and purified by the message I have given you. Remain in me, and I will remain in you.

—JOHN 15:1–4

Jesus is explaining that our connection to Him allows us to receive the strength and life that come from Him. Through our connection to God we discover the parts of our lives that aren't bearing fruit and learn what we need to prune—trim away, cut our connection to—in order to grow healthier and more productive. This is where we find the next "I am" declaration:

> For a branch cannot produce fruit if it is severed from the vine, and you cannot be fruitful unless you remain in me. Yes, *I am the vine*; you are the branches. Those who remain in me, and I in them, will produce much fruit. For apart from me you can do nothing. Anyone who does not remain in me is thrown away like a useless branch and withers. Such branches are gathered into a pile to be burned. But if you remain in me and my words remain in you, you may ask for anything you want, and it will be granted! When you produce much fruit, you are my true disciples. This brings great glory to my Father.
>
> —JOHN 15:4–8, EMPHASIS ADDED

Jesus wants us to understand that without this connection we won't be fruitful and healthy. If we aren't connected to Him, we will wither and die. That metaphor indicates that we won't produce in our lives without Him. But it also refers to a literal spiritual death because without that connection we will not spend eternity with Him in heaven.

But how do you become connected to God in the first place? Well, how do you build a connection with a person you want to know? When Martha and I met, I had just come out of a long season of searching for a wife and had finally surrendered myself to God's will for that part of my life. But if I hadn't actually introduced myself to Martha and started talking to her, we probably wouldn't be married today.

We built a strong relationship by spending time together and talking about all the things that were important to us. We shared ideas, memories, feelings, and experiences to learn more about each other. Martha and I eventually took the chance to open our hearts to each other. This is the same thing we have to do to build a connection with God.

We introduce ourselves and talk to Him (prayer), we spend time with Him (worship at church and on our own), we learn about Him (read His Word, the Bible), and we open our hearts to Him (surrender our lives to Him).

You might have a "lightning bolt moment" where you realize you want God in your life. That might cause you to get on fire for Him, and that is great. It's kind of like that love-at-first-sight feeling. But as with any human relationship, if you don't spend time cultivating it, the relationship won't thrive and be fruitful. You have to tend the vine of connection for it to be as strong as possible.

Building a Strong Connection

Being connected to God is about more than just a union; it's about communion with Him. When Martha and I got married, I thought, "This will be easy and awesome! As long as I've picked the right woman, this will be a piece of cake!"

We came from similar backgrounds. Our parents had been friends. We both had a passion for God and ministry. But it wasn't long into our marriage before I began asking, "Who is this woman?" And trust me, she was asking herself, "Who is this guy?"

We both realized our marriage was not playing out the way the fantasy did in our minds. We learned that relationships—real, lasting relationships—take work. We learned that communication is key for success. Whether good or bad, we found out we had to be honest about how we felt, and we had to encourage each other even when we didn't feel like it. We also had to pray and seek God together during tough times and believe Him for miracles.

Our marriage is not perfect, and sometimes we've had to fight to stay connected when things were difficult. But that is what has made our marriage so good. We have worked at being connected not just by a marriage license, but by communing with each other and with God in relationship. To be successful in marriage and any other significant relationship, you have to be led by God's Spirit and not your feelings.

Especially if a relationship is new, it can be hard to know how to build and strengthen it in a healthy way. Let's look at some important ways to nurture that kind of relationship.

Remain in His love.

Christianity—a relationship with God—is more than just saying a prayer of commitment. It's walking with Jesus every day. We have to remain in His love by spending time with Him in His Word and in prayer. Christianity is a love relationship with an awesome God.

Did you know the Bible is basically a love letter written to you? Look at these verses, which tell us just how much God loves us:

- **John 3:16**—"For God so loved the world that he gave his one and only Son, that whoever believes in him shall not perish but have eternal life" (NIV).

- **Romans 8:37–39**—"No, in all these things we are more than conquerors through him who loved us. For I am convinced that neither death nor life, neither angels nor demons, neither the present nor the future, nor any powers, neither height nor depth, nor anything else in all creation, will be able to separate us from the love of God that is in Christ Jesus our Lord" (NIV).

- **Ephesians 2:4–5**—"But God, being rich in mercy, because of His great love with which He loved us, even when we were dead in sins, made us alive together with Christ (by grace you have been saved)" (MEV).

- **Romans 5:8**—"But God shows his love for us in that while we were still sinners, Christ died for us" (ESV).

- **1 John 4:19**—"We love because he first loved us" (ESV).

- **1 Peter 5:6–7**—"Humble yourselves, therefore, under the mighty hand of God so that at the proper time he may exalt you, casting all your anxieties on him, because he cares for you" (ESV).

- **Psalm 86:15**—"But you, O Lord, are a God merciful and gracious, slow to anger and abounding in steadfast love and faithfulness" (ESV).

- **Galatians 2:20**—"I have been crucified with Christ. It is no longer I who live, but Christ who lives in me. And the life I now live in the flesh, I live by faith in the Son of God, who loved me and gave Himself for me" (MEV).

God loves us so deeply because He made us. He loves us so much that He sacrificed His Son to save us. His love for us is so great that He longs to have connection with us. When we have a love relationship with someone, we want to spend time with that person, and when we have a love relationship with Jesus, we should want to spend time with Him too.

How do we do that? We do it by spending time in His Word. God says we will be blessed and able to endure the challenges of life when we maintain and strengthen our connection with Him.

Obey His Word.

God has given us His Word not to hinder or restrict us, but to guide us into the life He planned for us. How do I know? He says so in His Word:

- **Jeremiah 29:11**—"'For I know the plans I have for you,' says the LORD. 'They are plans for good and not for disaster, to give you a future and a hope.'"

- **John 15:10**—"When you obey my commandments, you remain in my love, just as I obey my Father's commandments and remain in his love."

- **John 14:15**—"If you love me, you will keep my commandments" (ESV).

- **1 John 3:24**—"Whoever keeps his commandments abides in God, and God in him.
  And by this we know that he abides in us,
  by the Spirit whom he has given us" (esv).

- **John 8:51**—"Truly, truly, I say to you, if
  anyone keeps My word, he shall never see
  death" (mev).

You see, you have a heavenly Father who *loves* you! He
is *with* you, and He is *for* you!

The instruction God gives us in the Bible is no different from the rules you make for your children out of
a desire to see them healthy and safe. God has the benefit
of being able to see everything that lies ahead and how
it fits together with what is going on in the present and
what happened in the past. Because He has this perspective, the things He wants us to do and the way He wants
us to live are based on more knowledge and insight than
we have available. But we have to stay connected to Him
by knowing what He tells us in His Word if we want the
benefit of that wisdom.

Some of what we read in the Bible may seem restrictive, but it is all an expression of God's love. It is all for
our good. So we should revel in that connection with Him
instead of running away from it.

Enjoy the joy.

In the previous chapter we looked at what it means to
have more of God. One of the things it offers is more joy.

It might be easy to look at the obedience required by God as being restrictive and mean even though it is out of His love that He asks these things of us. But when we love God and are connected to Him, our love produces obedience, and obedience produces joy! That may sound strange to you, but look at how these verses explain what comes from our connection with God:

- **John 15:11**—"I have told you these things so that you will be filled with my joy. Yes, your joy will overflow!"

- **1 Peter 1:8**—"Though you have not seen him, you love him. Though you do not now see him, you believe in him and rejoice with joy that is inexpressible and filled with glory" (ESV).

- **Psalm 16:11**—"You make known to me the path of life; in your presence there is fullness of joy; at your right hand are pleasures forevermore" (ESV).

- **Romans 14:17**—"For the kingdom of God is not a matter of eating and drinking but of righteousness and peace and joy in the Holy Spirit" (ESV).

Joy in the Lord comes from our connection with Him, but we can't be in true communion and have a strong connection if we are not following His Word and trusting His leadership. Joy comes from having faith that He is with us always and that we can trust Him to lead us through whatever we are facing.

Sometimes that means trusting Him to shape us and different parts of our lives that may not be bearing fruit. Remember, some things bring temporary happiness but don't actually offer lasting joy. God may choose to prune those parts of our lives so we can experience the fullness of His joy.

Allow His pruning.

A vineyard gardener knows that he has to cut back some of the branches so the vine will be healthier and more fruitful. Sometimes we go through difficulties, and even though we haven't sinned or done anything wrong, God is using that challenge to prune the parts of our lives that aren't bearing fruit, and that can be hard to go through. It can be especially hard when God is asking us to let go of things that we like. But God may see that while certain relationships or behaviors aren't causing harm at the moment, they aren't producing healthy things in our lives either, and that will eventually have a negative impact on our overall growth.

Here's the good news: this is all part of God's plan for you to succeed and thrive in life. These verses explain how:

- **John 15:16**—"You didn't choose me. I chose you. I appointed you to go and produce lasting fruit, so that the Father will give you whatever you ask for, using my name."

- **Romans 11:17**—"But some of these branches from Abraham's tree—some of the people of Israel—have been broken off. And you Gentiles, who were branches from a wild olive tree, have been grafted in. So now you also receive the blessing God has promised Abraham and his children, sharing in the rich nourishment from the root of God's special olive tree."

Pruning is God's way of shaping us into the most fruitful and productive versions of ourselves. It allows Him to clear away what is not going to be useful to us. But it isn't enough to trim away branches that aren't useful. If you've ever done any pruning on a bush or tree in your yard, you have probably found out that you can make mistakes and cut off the connection to the plant's nourishment. And pruning isn't enough to keep a plant healthy and strong. Plants need to be fed, and so do we. We can't be pruned by God if we are not connected to Him, and we also can't benefit from this shaping if we aren't building a relationship with Him where He can nourish and restore us.

Being connected to God is vital for our spiritual growth and our ability to fulfill our purpose. We also have to be connected to one another to be fed in other ways. The following is a letter I received from one of my church members at a time when I was feeling disconnected and discouraged. Knowing I had this incredible network of support helped me realize where my help comes from, and I was able to build a deeper connection with God and His people.

Matt W.'s Story
We All Are Connected Through Jesus's Love

Pastor Matt and Martha,

During C3's anniversary weekend you told the story of how when we were in our old facility you became a little discouraged and began to question whether you wanted to be a senior pastor, that it might be easier to just go back to being a youth leader.

First, Pastor Matt, thank you for being transparent with us. You and Martha are honest and share your trials and challenges with us, reminding us that you experience the same difficulties we do, that you are not immune. You went on to say how blessed you were that Martha reminded you that you "were called here"...to provide real hope for real people in a real world.

Pastor Matt, I was one of those "real people" who needed "real hope." I was recently saved, having re-devoted my life to Jesus...but I was still broken and needed a shepherd to help me learn how to experience the abundant life. My daughter, Taylor, and I began attending C3 in January 2004, and that is when my healing and personal growth began.

Wow! What an amazing journey. I could write ten pages or more about all the breakthroughs and blessings. But to highlight, Taylor accepted Christ here at C3 while my mom was still living, and we got to enjoy seeing her baptized by you in the old worship center. She and I learned what service was as we got plugged into ministry. We learned what it means to live with purpose. We learned to be givers rather than consumers. We learned to tithe obediently and to give sacrificially, which radically transformed our lives. We experienced firsthand that the world of the generous gets larger and not smaller....Sunday after Sunday, message after message, God healed and restored me.

I learned to be a godly parent and shepherd my daughter through middle school, high school, and college. I learned to be a godly husband so that when God brought Courtney into my life, I was prepared to love her as Christ loved the church.

Pastor Matt, you and Martha remained obedient to your calling here in Clayton. That obedience allowed you to partner with God and the Holy Spirit to transform my life through the Word. Each and every Sunday during worship

I close my eyes and thank God for the people who provided that transformation...and you and Martha for answering that call and coming to Johnston County for *me*, for my real hope in my real world! My story is just one of countless stories, Pastor Matt. My life has, in turn, impacted countless others as I sow seed into the kingdom, as I learned through C3, with my time, my talent, and my treasure.

The ripple effect of your pressing in goes around the world. Please be encouraged...that the call you and Martha answered has produced life-changing fruit with generational impact! My family is blessed to have been transformed.

We love you both! God bless, and thank you for pressing in and answering the call!

I couldn't ask for a better illustration of how our individual connection to God yields fruit in our lives that impacts those around us, creating connections with others and strengthening all of us as we grow in Him. If you want the kind of life that is thriving and healthy, begin establishing your connection to the "vine" and to others who are growing in Him.

NEXT STEPS

Read John 15:7–8:

> If you remain in me and my words remain in you,
> ask whatever you wish, and it will be done for you.
> This is to my Father's glory, that you bear much
> fruit, showing yourselves to be my disciples.
>
> —NIV

Reflect:

- What does this passage say will happen if
  God's Word remains in you?

- What are some things you can do for God's
  Word to remain in you?

- Why do you think it is important to remain
  in God?

Declare:

> *God, You want a relationship with me. You
> know me and love me. I trust You with all my
> needs, and I can ask You anything. I can bear
> much fruit and live a fruitful life.*

Chapter Eight

Do You Know Who You Are?

I Am Who God Says I Am

Therefore, if anyone is in Christ, he
is a new creation. The old has passed
away; behold, the new has come.
—2 Corinthians 5:17, esv

IN THE INTRODUCTION I shared with you about the identity crisis I experienced when I lost the job I had at a church. I felt lost and alone. My entire sense of worth was determined by the position I held, and my identity was wrapped up in the title I carried. It took my being stripped of all that to realize none of it created my value. I discovered in those lowest moments that who I am is a child of God—that I am who He made me to be.

I've experienced the power of discovering who I am in

Christ and then declaring who I am. It took a while for me to realize my true identity in Christ, and it is definitely something I still have to remind myself of from time to time. The same may be true of you. At times we may deal with insecurity and doubt, but when we find our identity in Him, we struggle less to feel worthy because we don't have to question that God loves us. No matter how much money we have or how successful we are, no matter how famous we are or how many friends we have on Facebook, and no matter how much we do in life or how many lives we touch, God's deep love for us does not change.

Finding my identity in God opened up a lot of doors of opportunity and resolved the fears that were almost paralyzing me. But the greatest thing it did was help me discover who He made me to be and bring me into closer relationship with Him. Are you asking yourself, "Who am I?" If so, you have to start answering that question by understanding who God is and what He has done for you. That is what we've been exploring in this book. Once you know who He is, you will begin to find the answer to who you are.

WHERE DO YOU FIND YOUR IDENTITY?

It is a significant thing to have an identity—to be identified. We spend a large part of our lives seeking the kind of security and validation that comes from being identified with the popular group, the right company, or the perfect partner.

As children we cling to our parents or other family members when we are in unfamiliar places or around strangers.

You've probably seen children wrap their arms around their parents, holding on for dear life. They do that because it gives them a sense of safety to know their mom or dad is right there with them.

When we are teenagers, *everything* is about belonging—fitting in. It's so important to us that we make some pretty stupid mistakes and take some crazy risks trying to achieve that status. You can probably think of something you did as a teen to get noticed or liked that you would never consider now.

Once we reach young adulthood, our focus is on finding ourselves and solidifying our identity. We might get involved with groups or movements, hoping they will give us a sense of connection and protection. Unfortunately, in most cases the sense of security they offer is going to come up short. Sometimes it will be a total facade. It may be something as simple as believing a celebrity who endorses a product, only to discover it doesn't deliver on what was promised. Or it could be that you trusted the wrong person, and he or she ended up breaking your heart. Or it may be even more life altering, such as a false teaching you believed that led you away from what you knew to be true.

Establishing our identity is important to all of us. It's what allows us to rent a car, travel, hold a job, or get married. But the proof of identification I'll be talking about in this chapter is even more important than what you need to get into a government building, onto an airplane, or into a club. It's more valuable than a backstage pass at a concert.

I'm talking about the all-access pass to heaven that Jesus offers. It's the ultimate "I'm with Him!"

We have spent the last few chapters digging into who Jesus is. But other than the fact that He is God, why is it important to understand Jesus as the great I Am? It's because there is a direct connection between our view of God and how we see ourselves. In the introduction I stated that when we have a fresh encounter with the great I Am, that's when we discover who we are. The reason a fresh encounter with God is so impactful is because God made us, and He knows us better than we know ourselves. If we aren't connecting with Him in a real and personal way, we are missing out on really knowing who we are and who we were made to be.

By learning more about the person God intends for us to become, we begin to discover our purpose in life. That allows us to come into alignment with the plans God has for us. God designed each of us to fulfill certain accomplishments that come together to complete His work here.

Ultimately our primary pursuit here on earth is to share the love of Jesus with everyone we can in a real and practical way. My prayer is that my friends and family will spend eternity together with me in heaven. God has given each of us a purpose, and He chooses us to make a difference. Everything we do in this life is moving us toward that end. When we declare who we are in Christ, we invite God's blessings into our lives, and we open doors of opportunity for reaching others.

In Matthew 16:13–19 Jesus met with His disciples and

asked them, "Who do men say that I, the Son of Man, am?" (NKJV). They answered Him with, "Some say John the Baptist, some Elijah, and others Jeremiah or one of the prophets" (NKJV).

Then He asked them who they say He is. Peter said He was the Christ, the Son of the living God. When he did that, Jesus declared three things over him. He said Peter was blessed, that Peter was the foundation upon which He would build His church, and that he would receive the keys to the kingdom. All of this was true for Peter because he understood who Jesus was. When we gain that same understanding, God will speak the same over us. When we encounter the great I Am, we discover who we are!

Let's see what we can learn about who we are from what Jesus told Peter.

We are blessed.

Jesus told Peter: "You are blessed, Simon son of John, because my Father in heaven has revealed this to you. You did not learn this from any human being" (Matt. 16:17). We too are blessed. But what does that mean?

Blessed is a term a lot of people throw around these days, but not everyone truly understands what it means to be blessed by God. James 1:12 says, "God blesses those who patiently endure testing and temptation. Afterward they will receive the crown of life that God has promised to those who love him."

Often when people think of God's blessing, they think of a financial blessing. But God's blessings have to do with much more than our income. God wants to bless us with things money can't buy, such as the peace of God during a difficult time, the joy He gives that provides strength during the storms of life, the blessing of your children's knowing God and making a difference with their lives, or the blessing of knowing that generations coming behind you are impacted by your life choices. Those are some of the greatest blessings of all! I've discovered that when I focus on putting God first and giving Him my heart, I don't worry about how God might bless me.

If we do not understand who Christ is and how much He loves us—if we don't get what it really means to be blessed—we might think God has removed His blessing from our lives whenever we experience conflict or difficulty. And those who have struggled throughout their lives may feel God has never blessed them. We would think that because we are defining blessing in worldly terms. We are under the mistaken impression that the temporary things of this life are the only ways God shows His love to us.

God does want to meet all our needs, but He is more concerned with making sure we are blessed spiritually. He empowers us with the strength and endurance to overcome whatever challenges we face in the world. He gives us the comfort and peace of knowing that every difficulty we must endure will pass and that He will use them to prepare for future opportunities. He covers us with His love and grace, which takes the edge off the hardships we may face, and He has secured our eternity in heaven with Him through His sacrifice on the cross.

Blessings come in a lot of forms, and we don't always recognize them when we are experiencing them because we are too focused on the here and now. Knowing who you are in Jesus is an important part of being able to identify and cling to the blessings in your life even when it appears from the outside that things aren't going well.

We get to build His church.

When we understand how we are blessed and realize who Christ is, we discover the importance of His church for us and everyone we encounter. We realize the role it plays in our growth and what a privilege it is to be a part of building that church here on earth.

The church is not a building; it's people. The church is not just a place to show up at on Sundays; it's a nurturing community. We are the church, and when we understand who we are in Christ and all He has done for us, our passion becomes sharing the good news of Jesus and building His church. When we understand that Jesus really is the Christ, the Son of the living God, and that He died for us, our response is that we want to change the world through the local church.

But I want to be clear: the church Jesus referred to is not a single denomination. Remember, when Jesus's disciples were gathering His followers and sharing the gospel, most cities didn't have more than one church. In fact, denominations didn't start developing until about a thousand years after Jesus's death and resurrection. They are entirely man-made and often used as a means to bring division among the church instead of celebrating the many ways God creatively uses His church to reach the lost. We should remain united as one body in Christ no matter our denominational background as we worship an awesome and holy God.

The local church is the hope of the world. It is where we find support for our spiritual lives, leadership as we learn more about who God is, healing from the difficulties of life, and celebration of the victories over our struggles. Many people pull away from church because of bad experiences in the past, or they avoid churches because they either don't know what to expect or have heard horror stories from people who left the church. I want to encourage anyone who is not involved in a local church to try again. Visit a church in your area, and find one where you can start making a difference. Giving up one Sunday isn't a big commitment when you consider what a great gift this kind of support system can be for your life.

If you are part of a church family but aren't involved and serving, you are missing out on some of what God wants to do in your life. God did not ask us to build His church just so we'd have a place to go to sing and hear someone talk for a little while on Sunday mornings. God created us to live in community with other believers and to live out His purpose for our lives. Get involved, and get to know the people around you in the church, and together you can make a difference. You will discover a deeper relationship with God as you build relationships with other believers.

At C3 Church, we have an army of volunteers we call the "Dream Team." There are hundreds of people who use their gifts and talents each week while serving on various ministry teams. It's amazing to see them week after week cheerfully parking cars, setting up chairs, leading us in worship, teaching our kids, and serving coffee in our café. God blesses us when we have a "want to" attitude and not a "have to" attitude. When we do this, we get to build His church!

He gives us the keys to the kingdom.

The final thing Jesus declared over Peter was that he would be given the keys to the kingdom. I believe the key to unlocking the kingdom of God is discovering who we are and then declaring who God says we are.

I believe God wants us to experience a taste of heaven here on earth. This is why Jesus prayed, "Thy kingdom come, Thy will be done in earth, as it is in heaven" (Matt. 6:10, KJV). But how can we make this a reality in our lives?

First, it is important to understand what God's kingdom is. In our world today we don't have many kingdoms. But when I traveled to Swaziland in Africa, for example, there was a king. The king is the most powerful person in the country and has almost unlimited resources. We see an example in the Bible, in Acts 3, of the power of a kingdom, where a man who had been lame since birth was begging for money outside the temple gate. Peter walked by and reached out to him:

> Then Peter said, "Silver or gold I do not have, but what I do have I give you. In the name of Jesus Christ of Nazareth, walk." Taking him by the right hand, he helped him up, and instantly the

man's feet and ankles became strong. He jumped
to his feet and began to walk. Then he went with
them into the temple courts, walking and jumping,
and praising God.

—Acts 3:6–8, niv

Notice Peter declared, "In the name of Jesus"! In that
culture calling forth a person's name meant you were
calling on his power and authority. For example, if an offi-
cial said, "In the name of Caesar," it meant the power of
the emperor and all of his kingdom could be brought to
bear on that particular situation.

Our name represents our reputation and authority. A
more modern example is how when my mom said something, I knew I'd better listen. And if she said, "Wait till
your dad gets home," I knew I was in serious trouble. What
Dad said and did was another level. We might have to consider what our bosses say or what the president said. But
when you declare something "in the name of Jesus," all
the power of our God and His kingdom will be brought
to bear on your situation! When you pray in the name
of Jesus, the name that is above every name, you put His
power and His purpose to work!

So having the keys to the kingdom means that whatever
we bind on earth will be bound in heaven, and whatever
we loose on earth will be loosed in heaven. (See Matthew
18:18.) That means what we say has a huge impact on our
lives because whatever we ask for in Jesus's name according
to His will can happen. We really have to know God to

know what He wants for our lives so we can unleash what heaven wants us to experience in this life.

Knowing who we are in God is powerful, and using it in a way that honors Him and helps bring His will to completion is our greatest responsibility. Now that we have talked about the significance of what it means to know who we are and what can come of it, let's get a little more specific about what God tells us in the Bible about who we are.

WHO ARE YOU?

How would you finish the sentence "I am..."?

The way you finish that "I am" statement will determine your future because whatever you say has an impact on your future. Think about what would happen if you told yourself:

- I am stupid.

- I am slow.

- I am ugly.

- I am no good.

- I am an idiot.

- I am worn out.

How do those statements make you feel? Do they uplift and encourage you? Or do they make you feel small and unlovable? If you see yourself in negative terms, those ideas will prevent you from being effective in every aspect of your life and keep you from being everything God made you to be.

Proverbs 18:21 tells us, "The tongue has the power of life and death, and those who love it will eat its fruit" (NIV). When we make unflattering statements about ourselves, we invite the power of that negativity into our lives. We should be sending out invitations such as these instead:

- I am made in the image of God.

- I am God's masterpiece.

- I am fearfully and wonderfully made.

- I am loved.

- I am wanted.

- I am blessed.

Unfortunately, being positive and hopeful seems to go against human nature. Most of us think we are just average. We focus on what we can't do instead of what God specifically designed us to do.

Do you realize that there is nothing ordinary about any of us? We are all made to be unique. There is not another you. There is not another me. Each of us is an original. Even twins aren't completely identical. One of the most important parts of discovering who we are in Christ is the realization that we were made individually for a specific purpose. When we know this, we understand that we have a destiny to fulfill, and none of those negative messages have any impact on us. We can stop comparing what we have with what others have because it is irrelevant. We have what we need to do the very special and very exclusive things God designed us to do.

In Genesis 17:15–21 we learn about Sarai and Abraham, who became impatient as they waited for God to give them the child He promised. Sarai couldn't become pregnant, and in that era women were looked down on if they couldn't give birth.

Sarai lost sight of God's goodness and faithfulness. She gave her maid to Abraham in an attempt to find her own way of bringing God's promise to pass. She stopped trusting God's word to her and Abraham. She lost hope after listening to her own fears and the messages of the enemy that told her she was a failure in this and God couldn't use her. But even after she turned on God, He still changed her name from Sarai to Sarah, which means "princess," to show her that He had not changed His mind about her or stopped loving her. He wanted her and Abraham to know that He still intended to keep His promise and help them fulfill the destiny He planned for them.

Names carried significant meanings in biblical times and could have a huge effect on both how those individuals were perceived in their communities and how they saw themselves. God is really big on changing names to help us change our hearts and the way we see ourselves. He did it with Sarah's husband, Abraham. He also did it when He changed Jacob's name to Israel (Gen. 35:10), Simon to Peter (Matt. 16:18–19), and Saul to Paul (Acts 9:1–19; 13:9–11).

So when God changed Sarai's name to signify something special, she heard Him calling her Princess over and over, and that began to change her self-image. She went from telling herself, "I am a failure," to believing, "I am a princess." After this Sarah and Abraham welcomed their son, Isaac, into the world and experienced their destiny.

Our words have power—power over how we see ourselves, how others see us, how we see others, and how we see God. It is important to speak words of life because it is through our words that we either shut God out of our lives or invite Him in to do amazing things.

Know What You Are and What You Are Not

Sometimes the harmful messages we tell ourselves don't take the form of a negative statement—"I am not good enough; I am not likable; I am not smart"—but still have a negative tone. Sometimes we need to hear what we are not in order to understand all the amazing things that we are in God. These declarations from the Bible reject the disabling thoughts that keep us distracted. This list of "I Am Nots" will equip and empower you to stand up against the messages the enemy uses to tear you down.

I Am Nots

- When the enemy says God doesn't care about you, tell him, "I am not forsaken." (See Hebrews 13:5.)

- When the enemy says God isn't paying attention to your needs, tell him, "I am not forgotten." (See Isaiah 49:15.)

- When the enemy says you are all alone, tell him, "I am not abandoned." (See Hebrews 13:5.)

- When the enemy says nobody wants you, tell him, "I am not rejected." (See Ephesians 1:6.)

- When the enemy says you have nothing to offer, tell him, "I am not useless." (See Ephesians 2:10.)

- When the enemy says you can't do anything right, tell him, "I am not helpless." (See Psalm 121:2.)

- When the enemy says you might as well give up, tell him, "I am not hopeless." (See Romans 15:13.)

- When the enemy says God will never forgive you, tell him, "I am not condemned." (See Romans 8:1.)

- When the enemy says you've got it all wrong, tell him, "I am not confused." (See 1 Corinthians 14:33.)

- When the enemy says there's no way out, tell him, "I am not destroyed." (See Isaiah 43:1–2.)

- When the enemy says you have nothing more to give, tell him, "I am not desolate." (See John 15:5.)

- When the enemy says God is not going to be there for you, tell him, "I am not deserted." (See John 14:18.)

- When the enemy says you are not important to God, tell him, "I am not uncared for." (See 1 Peter 5:7.)

- When the enemy says God is not looking out for you, tell him, "I am not unprotected." (See Psalm 3:3.)

- When the enemy says no one really likes you, tell him, "I am not unwanted." (See Luke 19:10.)

- When the enemy says you are insignificant, tell him, "I am not unknown." (See Isaiah 43:1.)

- When the enemy says you are not worthy, tell him, "I am not unloved." (See Jeremiah 31:3.)

As you learn how to reject the hurtful messages, it is just as important to begin embracing God's powerful truth as well. Begin declaring the promises God gives us in the Bible. God in His infinite wisdom chose to make you the way He did for a very specific purpose. Know that God does not make mistakes and has very special plans for your life that are uniquely yours.

Michelle's Story
I Am Changed and Redeemed

My story began in a small classroom in our church in Worthington, Virginia. I can remember repeating the words my teacher spoke as I asked Jesus into my heart. I was four years old.

I have always loved church life. On each side of my family I am either the third or fourth generation in ministry. The first time I ever led a class, I was twelve years old. My dad called me to the five-year-olds class, handed me a book, told me what to read, and left me to teach the class. That was the beginning of many years of serving alongside my dad in ministry.

While I loved serving in the church and loved God with all my heart, there was a dark side I kept hidden for a very long time. I was the victim of several forms of abuse by various people. At age five I was exposed to sexual acts that left me feeling broken and unworthy. As a teen I was involved in a couple of relationships where I allowed myself to be abused emotionally and physically. I was living two lives that were on a collision course. I used my church life to hide from my hurt and allowed it to become my identity.

After years of hiding the pain, it began to wear on my physical body. I suffered from terrible back spasms that would leave me unable to move for weeks. In the spring of 2007 I suffered the worst one I had ever had, but it was during this time that God started my healing process. I spent countless hours praying and seeking God for healing. One afternoon while I was praying, God showed me a vision of my husband, Dan, and me standing in a worship service in a church I had never seen. In that moment He said, "Michelle, the day is coming when I am going to ask you to leave your father's ministry. So get ready." I honestly thought that would be a few months away at the most, but it wasn't until the winter of 2011 when God finally told us it was time. Little did I know, it would be the hardest thing I'd ever had to do.

I showed up that first Sunday to C3 Church broken, scared, and feeling so alone. I had been stripped of my security and my identity all at once. For weeks I would stare up at the people on stage with tears streaming down my face, thinking, "Does anyone see my pain? Does anyone hear me screaming?" I joined a connect group and soon found a group of friends I could lean on. It wasn't long before I started taking the biblical discipleship class and began unpacking some of the overwhelming feelings I struggled with. I began serving as a teacher in the preschool ministry and found a lot of joy there. Still there was something missing. There was still a hurt so deep within me that I couldn't quite grab onto it.

A year after joining the preschool ministry team, I came on staff as the director of the preschool ministry. I was so happy to be back in ministry, but I also knew God was positioning me for something more. It wasn't long before I found myself in a C3 connect group called Reality Revealed, where years of hurt and abuse began to melt away in the light of God's grace. Then God began to teach me about who I am in Him through our freedom groups. In those two groups God gave me a new security and identity, grounded in His love.

A lot has happened in the two years since I have been on staff. I am not the same person I was when I came to C3 Church. God has used this house, its teachings, and its leaders to set this captive free. I am so thankful for the freedom I have found here. And I am looking forward to my best days as I enter a new phase of the journey as the children's minister of C3 Kids. I am excited to see how God can use my freedom to serve the next generation!

It's not enough to reject the negative or hurtful messages the enemy would have us believe about ourselves. We must be empowered by the positive messages God pours into our lives to shape our identity in Him. Fulfilling our purpose and discovering who we are in Christ is about more than just telling ourselves good things. We have to embrace God's promises, make them part of our lives, and begin actually living them out.

A couple of years ago Martha and I were facing a very difficult time. We kept running into a brick wall while trying to deal with some situations that were beyond our control. In one situation we needed a financial miracle. We had two girls in college, and we just needed something supernatural to happen in our finances as well as in some other areas. We began to declare the promises of God every day. We would join hands in prayer each day and declare God's promises over our lives and over our situation. It was amazing how we immediately began to feel more faith rise up. We experienced more peace in our hearts, and during that season of declaring God's promises every day—whether we felt like it or not—God began to give us miracles that turned our situation around.

One specific miracle was when we needed to find a particular document to prove my ordination. The certificate had been lost in years of files we had stored away, and it wasn't something we could just find online and reprint. It was like finding a needle in a haystack, but Martha happened to go into the attic and found this sheet of paper that ended up saving us tens of thousands of dollars.

This supernatural breakthrough showed us just how powerful declaring the promises of God can be. When we declare who we are in Christ and declare to Him who He is and what He can do in our lives, breakthrough comes and brings blessings with it.

The following "I am" declarations are the best map to guide you as you seek to step into the purpose God has designed for your life. Let's use these thirty-one "I am" declarations daily to speak freedom over our lives, in Jesus's name. By doing so, instead of looking to your own power to change your situation, you will be looking to the power found in Jesus—the only power that can transform your life.

NEXT STEPS

For the next thirty-one days, I challenge you to declare the following statements over your life and circumstances every day. As you do, you will begin to see things from God's perspective. And as you begin to see from God's perspective, your life will begin to change. I believe you will see breakthroughs and miracles that can't be explained on paper. God is waiting for us to trust Him for the impossible as we declare what He says about us. And I've discovered that even if my circumstances don't change, when I declare who God is, I have a strength and a confidence that my God is bigger than anything I am going through. And that gives me a peace beyond human comprehension.

So take some time each day and declare these truths. The more you say them, the more real they will become to you. And when that happens, when the truth of these declarations really gets down in your heart, your life will never be the same. Knowing I Am changes everything.

YOUR "I AM" DECLARATIONS

I am fearfully and wonderfully made by a holy God.

Thank you for making me so wonderfully complex! Your workmanship is marvelous—how well I know it.

—Psalm 139:14

Thank You, God, that I am not an accident. You knit me in my mother's womb. I am fearfully and wonderfully made by the Creator of the universe.

I am God's masterpiece.

For we are God's masterpiece. He has created us anew in Christ Jesus, so we can do the good things he planned for us long ago.

—Ephesians 2:10

I thank You, God, that I was handcrafted by You. There is no one else in the world exactly like me. I am one of a kind, and I have a destiny.

I am made in the image of God.

Then God said, "Let us make human beings in our image, to be like us. They will reign over the fish in the sea, the birds in the sky, the livestock, all the wild animals on the earth, and the small animals that scurry along the ground."

—Genesis 1:26; also see Genesis 9:6;
Colossians 1:27

I thank You, God, that I was made in Your image! And Your Word says in John 14:12 that we can do even greater things than You ever did!

I am forgiven.

And he ordered us to preach everywhere and to testify that Jesus is the one appointed by God to be the judge of all—the living and the dead. He is the one all the prophets testified about, saying that everyone who believes in him will have their sins forgiven through his name.

—ACTS 10:42–43; ALSO SEE 1 JOHN 1:9; ISAIAH 43:25–26; PSALM 103:12

I thank You, God, that when we confess our sins to You, You forgive us, cleanse us, and forget about our wrongdoing! Our sins are washed away forever, and we can live in freedom.

I am redeemed by God.

In him we have redemption through his blood, the forgiveness of sins, in accordance with the riches of God's grace.

—EPHESIANS 1:7, NIV

I thank You, God, that You have redeemed my life and have given me a fresh start!

I am called by name.

But now, O Jacob, listen to the LORD who created you. O Israel, the one who formed you says,

"Do not be afraid, for I have ransomed you. I have called you by name; you are mine."

—Isaiah 43:1

I thank You, God, that You know my name. Not only do you save me, but You also call me to make a difference! I thank You that I can have a relationship with You that is real and personal.

I am a new creation—the old life is gone!

This means that anyone who belongs to Christ has become a new person. The old life is gone; a new life has begun!

—2 Corinthians 5:17;
also see Colossians 3:10

I thank You, God, that I am a new creation. You are the only One who can create and make new. I declare that my old life is gone and You are doing a new thing in my life!

I am greatly loved by God.

This is real love—not that we loved God, but that he loved us and sent his Son as a sacrifice to take away our sins.

—1 John 4:10

I thank You, God, that You love me unconditionally, with no strings attached. You love me no matter who I am or what I've done. You love me even when I don't deserve it.

I am His child.

See how very much our Father loves us, for he calls us his children, and that is what we are! But the people who belong to this world don't recognize that we are God's children because they don't know him. Dear friends, we are already God's children, but he has not yet shown us what we will be like when Christ appears. But we do know that we will be like him, for we will see him as he really is.

—1 JOHN 3:1–2; ALSO SEE ROMANS 8:14–15

I thank You, God, that I am a child of the most high God! I don't have to live in fear because I know that You are my heavenly Father.

I am an heir of God and coheir with Christ.

And since we are his children, we are his heirs. In fact, together with Christ we are heirs of God's glory. But if we are to share his glory, we must also share his suffering.

—ROMANS 8:17; ALSO SEE GALATIANS 3:29

I thank You, God, that I inherit everything of Your kingdom as a child of God.

I am a member of God's family.

So now you Gentiles are no longer strangers and foreigners. You are citizens along with all of God's holy people. You are members of God's family.

Together, we are his house, built on the foundation of the apostles and the prophets. And the cornerstone is Christ Jesus himself.

—Ephesians 2:19–20;
also see Ephesians 3:15, mev

I thank You, God, that I am not alone but that I belong to Your family.

I am blessed in the heavenly realm with every spiritual blessing.

All praise to God, the Father of our Lord Jesus Christ, who has blessed us with every spiritual blessing in the heavenly realms because we are united with Christ.

—Ephesians 1:3

Thank You, God, for blessing me with every spiritual blessing!

I am chosen to be part of a royal priesthood, a holy nation set apart for God.

But you are not like that, for you are a chosen people. You are royal priests, a holy nation, God's very own possession. As a result, you can show others the goodness of God, for he called you out of the darkness into his wonderful light.

—1 Peter 2:9; also see Revelation 5:10;
Ephesians 1:3–4

Thank You, God, for choosing me to be royalty.

I am His treasured possession.

"Now if you will obey me and keep my covenant, you will be my own special treasure from among all the peoples on earth; for all the earth belongs to me. And you will be my kingdom of priests, my holy nation." This is the message you must give to the people of Israel.

—EXODUS 19:5–6; ALSO SEE 2 CORINTHIANS 4:7

I thank You, God, that I have value in Your eyes and I am Your treasured possession.

I am precious to God. I am being built into a spiritual house.

You are coming to Christ, who is the living cornerstone of God's temple. He was rejected by people, but he was chosen by God for great honor. And you are living stones that God is building into his spiritual temple. What's more, you are his holy priests. Through the mediation of Jesus Christ, you offer spiritual sacrifices that please God.

—1 PETER 2:4–5

I thank You, God, that You don't see me as just a number, but as someone who is precious to You.

I am a temple of the living God.

Don't you realize that all of you together are the temple of God and that the Spirit of God lives in you? God will destroy anyone who destroys this temple. For God's temple is holy, and you are that temple.

—1 Corinthians 3:16–17; also see
1 Corinthians 6:19; 2 Corinthians 6:16

Thank You, God, that my body is Your temple. I declare that I will keep it healthy for Your glory.

I am full and complete, lacking nothing.

For in Christ lives all the fullness of God in a human body. So you also are complete through your union with Christ, who is the head over every ruler and authority.

—Colossians 2:9–10; also see 2 Peter 1:3

I thank You, God, that You are not just the God of enough, but You are the God of more than enough! I declare that You are an "above and beyond" God, and I will live an "above and beyond" life for You.

I am the righteousness of God.

For God made Christ, who never sinned, to be the offering for our sin, so that we could be made right with God through Christ.

—2 Corinthians 5:21

I thank You, God, that You see me as righteous and holy because of what You did for me on the cross.

I am His ambassador.

And all of this is a gift from God, who brought us back to himself through Christ. And God has given us this task of reconciling people to him. For God was in Christ, reconciling the world to himself, no longer counting people's sins against them. And he gave us this wonderful message of reconciliation. So we are Christ's ambassadors; God is making his appeal through us. We speak for Christ when we plead, "Come back to God!"

—2 Corinthians 5:18–20

I thank You, God, that I have the privilege of being Your ambassador, sharing Your love and good news with the world.

I am free.

So if the Son sets you free, you are truly free.

—John 8:36; also see Galatians 5:1;
Romans 8:2

I thank You, God, that I no longer live in past regret and failure, but You have set me free to have an amazing future.

I am healed.

He forgives all my sins and heals all my diseases.

—Psalm 103:3

I thank You, God, that because of what You have done for me, I can be healed spiritually, physically, and emotionally.

I am whole.

He personally carried our sins in his body on the cross so that we can be dead to sin and live for what is right. By his wounds you are healed.
—1 Peter 2:24; also see Mark 10:52, kjv; Acts 3:16

I thank You, God, that I am a whole and complete person. I declare that Christ is enough for me.

I am more than a conqueror.

No, in all these things we are more than conquerors through Him who loved us.
—Romans 8:37, mev; also see 1 Corinthians 15:57

I thank You, God, that I am more than a conqueror and have power over the enemy, in Jesus's name. Nothing can stop me from living out Your plan for my life.

I am a warrior for Christ.

Endure suffering along with me, as a good soldier of Christ Jesus. Soldiers don't get tied up in the affairs of civilian life, for then they cannot please the officer who enlisted them.
—2 Timothy 2:3–4; also see Psalm 18:32–42

I thank You, God, that I am a mighty warrior for You. I declare that I will fight the good fight through prayer and by shining Your light to others.

I am wanted.

Come close to God, and God will come close to you. Wash your hands, you sinners; purify your hearts, for your loyalty is divided between God and the world.

—JAMES 4:8

I thank You, God, that not only do You love me, but You also like me. You want me to be in Your presence. I declare that I will draw closer to You as You draw closer to me.

I am significant.

All of you together are Christ's body, and each of you is a part of it.

—1 CORINTHIANS 12:27;
ALSO SEE ROMANS 12:4–5

I thank You, God, that You didn't call me to live a normal life but give me the power to live a significant life for Your glory.

I am a citizen of God's kingdom.

Since we are receiving a Kingdom that is unshakable, let us be thankful and please God by worshiping him with holy fear and awe.

—HEBREWS 12:28; ALSO SEE PHILIPPIANS 3:20

I thank You, Lord, that this earth is not my home, but my eternal home is in heaven, and I am a citizen of Your kingdom!

I am sent by God.

As he spoke, he showed them the wounds in his hands and his side. They were filled with joy when they saw the Lord! Again he said, "Peace be with you. As the Father has sent me, so I am sending you." Then he breathed on them and said, "Receive the Holy Spirit. If you forgive anyone's sins, they are forgiven. If you do not forgive them, they are not forgiven."

—John 20:20–23; also see Romans 10:15

I thank You, God, for saving me and calling me to live my life on assignment from You to make a difference in the world.

I am light in the darkness.

You are the salt of the earth. But what good is salt if it has lost its flavor? Can you make it salty again? It will be thrown out and trampled underfoot as worthless. You are the light of the world—like a city on a hilltop that cannot be hidden. No one lights a lamp and then puts it under a basket. Instead, a lamp is placed on a stand, where it gives light to everyone in the house. In the same way, let your good deeds shine out for all to see, so that everyone will praise your heavenly Father.

—MATTHEW 5:13–16; ALSO SEE EPHESIANS 5:8

I thank You, God, that I can shine Your light in the dark places, and because of Your goodness to me others will see how awesome You are.

I am a friend of God, chosen by Him and appointed to bear good fruit.

I no longer call you slaves, because a master doesn't confide in his slaves. Now you are my friends, since I have told you everything the Father told me. You didn't choose me. I chose you. I appointed you to go and produce lasting fruit, so that the Father will give you whatever you ask for, using my name.

—JOHN 15:15–16

Lord, I thank You that I am a friend of Yours and that when I abide in You I will bear all of the fruit of the Spirit!

I am His radiant bride; I am without spot or wrinkle.

For husbands, this means love your wives, just as Christ loved the church. He gave up his life for her to make her holy and clean, washed by the cleansing of God's word. He did this to present her to himself as a glorious church without a spot or wrinkle or any other blemish. Instead, she will be holy and without fault. In the same way, husbands ought to love their wives as they love their own bodies. For a man who loves his wife actually shows love for himself. No one hates his own body but feeds and cares for it, just as Christ cares for the church. And we are members of his body. As the Scriptures say, "A man leaves his father and mother and is joined to his wife, and the two are united into one." This is a great mystery, but it is an illustration of the way Christ and the church are one.

—Ephesians 5:25–32;
also see 2 Corinthians 11:2

I thank You, God, that You are coming again for Your church and that as part of Your family I am a radiant bride who is clean and holy!

***

I want to share some personal thoughts as we conclude. I was raised in a Christian home and received Christ as a child. My dad shared the gospel with me in our home, and later He baptized me in the church he pastored in Tucson, Arizona. I have been walking with God for many years now, and as I look back, it's been an exciting journey. The Christian life is amazing, but it's a matter of walking day by day, step by step with God.

The principles I share in this book have come out of many decades of walking with God. And my journey with God continues! Take the principles from this book, and declare every day who you are in Christ and all that He wants to do in and through your life. As we discover and declare God's Word and His promises, we can live lives of purpose and peace in a crazy world.

Notes

Chapter Two
Do You Feel Lost?

1.   "Light Therapy," Mayo Clinic, accessed January 10, 2017, http://www.mayoclinic.org/tests-procedures/light-therapy/home/ovc-20197416.

2.   David Brickner, "Finding Jesus in the Feast of Tabernacles," CBN, accessed January 10, 2017, http://www1.cbn.com/finding-jesus-feast-tabernacles; see also commentaries on John 8:12, viewed at Bible Hub, accessed January 10, 2017, http://biblehub.com/commentaries/john/8-12.htm.

Chapter Five
Do You Need Power?

1.   *Strong's Exhaustive Concordance*, s.v. "G2222–zōē," viewed at Blue Letter Bible, accessed November 16, 2016, https://www.blueletterbible.org//lang/Lexicon/Lexicon.cfm?Strongs=G2222&t=KJV; see also Trench's New Testament Synonyms, s.v. "life," accessed November 16, 2016, http://studybible.info/trench/life.

Chapter Six
Do You Need More of God?

1.   For more information, see Lee Strobel's *The Case for Christ*, Josh McDowell's *Evidence That Demands a Verdict*, and Gary Habermas's *The Case for the Resurrection of Jesus* and *Did Jesus Rise From the Dead?* Gary Habermas, PhD, distinguished professor and chair of the Department of Philosophy and Theology at Liberty University, in communication with the author, fall 1983.

CONNECT WITH US!

CHARISMA HOUSE

(Spiritual Growth)

f Facebook.com/CharismaHouse

🐦 @CharismaHouse

📷 Instagram.com/CharismaHouse

SILOAM

(Health)

📌 Pinterest.com/CharismaHouse

MEV MODERN ENGLISH VERSION

(Bible)

www.mevbible.com